DELIA EPHRON

Funny Sauce

US,
THE EX,
THE EX'S NEW MATE,
THE NEW MATE'S EX,
AND THE
KIDS

VIKING

VIKING
Viking Penguin Inc., 40 West 23rd Street,
New York, New York 10010, U.S.A.
Penguin Books Ltd, Harmondsworth,
Middlesex, England
Penguin Books Australia Ltd, Ringwood,
Victoria, Australia
Penguin Books Canada Limited, 2801 John Street,
Markham, Ontario, Canada L3R 1B4
Penguin Books (N.Z.) Ltd, 182–190 Wairau Road,
Auckland 10, New Zealand

Copyright © Delia Ephron, 1982, 1983, 1986
All rights reserved

First published in 1986 by Viking Penguin Inc.
Published simultaneously in Canada

Some of the essays in this book were previously published as follows: "Trixie" under the title "The Morbid Age," "The Toy," and "B-E-V-E-R-L-Y" in *California Magazine*, "Mom in Love" in *Redbook*, "Some Famous Couples Discuss Their Divorces" in *Esquire*, "Coping with Santa" and "I Am the Green Lollipop: Notes on Stepmothering" in *The New York Times*.

Grateful acknowledgment is made
for permission to reprint the following copyrighted material:

Excerpt from "Send in the Clowns" by Stephen Sondheim. © 1973, 1985 Revelation Music Publishing Corporation/Rilting Music Inc. A Tommy Valando Publication.

Excerpt from "People Will Say We're in Love" by Richard Rodgers and Oscar Hammerstein II. Copyright © 1943 by Williamson Music Co. Copyright renewed. International copyright secured. All rights reserved. Used by permission.

LIBRARY OF CONGRESS CATALOGING IN PUBLICATION DATA
Ephron, Delia.
Funny sauce.
1. Family—Anecdotes, facetiae, satire, etc.
I. Title.
PN6231.F3E74   1986   814'.54   85-41084
ISBN 0-670-81240-4

Printed in the United States of America by
Haddon Craftsmen, Scranton, Pennsylvania
Set in Garamond

Without limiting the rights under copyright reserved above, no part of this publication may be reproduced, stored in or introduced into a retrieval system, or transmitted, in any form or by any means (electronic, mechanical, photocopying, recording or otherwise), without the prior written permission of both the copyright owner and the above publisher of this book.

To the family I married into

*The accounts of my family life in this book are true.
I have changed all the names, however, except those
of the offspring of the famous and/or wealthy in the
chapter titled "B-E-V-E-R-L-Y."*

It occurred to me while writing this book that the extended family is in our lives again. This should make all the people happy who were complaining back in the sixties and seventies that the reason family life was so hard, especially on mothers, was that the nuclear family had replaced the extended family. No longer were there relatives on call to help raise the children.

We owe the return of the extended family, albeit in a slightly altered form, to an innovation called joint custody, in which two formerly married people share in raising their children. Your basic extended family today includes your ex-husband or -wife, your ex's new mate, your new mate, possibly your new mate's ex, and any new mate that your new mate's ex has acquired. It consists entirely of people who are not related by blood, many of whom can't stand each other. This return of the extended family reminds me of the favorite saying of my friend's extremely pessimistic mother: Be careful what you wish for, you might get it.

CONTENTS

·· CONTENTS ··

"I don't like chicken in funny sauce."

—stepchild to stepmother, c. 1984

Funny Sauce

Trixie

The story actually began a week earlier when my stepson, Alex, swallowed a marble. Alex was five, and he was playing with a clock that his father and I had bought at a garage sale. The clock had thirteen small metal marbles that slid down a chute and a complicated system of weights and balances. The number of marbles that were on the chute and the number that had dropped off told you the time if you knew how to calculate it. Which we didn't. We bought the clock only because it cost two dollars and Alex was fascinated with the way the marbles dropped. Apparently he was more fascinated with marbles than we realized because he walked into the living room and announced that he had swallowed one. Slightly hysterical, we called the doctor. He said, since Alex was not choking, there was nothing to worry about—the marble would come out eventually when he went to the bathroom.

Enter Lisa, Alex's eight-year-old sister. I found her and Alex in the bathroom, where Lisa was trying to convince Alex to "go" so she could see the marble come out. I explained that the marble would not show up for a day or two at least, and they should not worry about it. Then I repeated that Alex should never, never, never swallow a marble again because it could get stuck in his throat.

Five minutes later Lisa and Alex were back in the living room, and Lisa announced that Alex could feel the marble in his throat. "Is this the truth?" his dad asked. Alex nodded. We bundled them into the car and headed for the hospital.

At the emergency room the doctor asked Alex, "Where's the marble?" and Lisa showed him, pointing to the center front of Alex's throat. I said, "Lisa, let Alex tell the doctor. Alex, where's the marble?" Alex pointed to the place Lisa had pointed to.

We were fortunate, the doctor explained, because Alex had not swallowed a glass marble but a metal marble, which would show up nicely in an x-ray. So Alex was x-rayed while Lisa tried to sneak into an examining room where an elderly man lay in what looked like cardiac arrest. I scolded her and looked somewhat abashedly at the doctor who had stopped her. "She's at the morbid age," he said, and laughed.

Alex's marble appeared in the x-ray somewhere in his upper intestine, safely on its way to being expelled. We went home.

A week later. I was helping Alex construct a model of *Tyrannosaurus rex* when the screen door crashed open, slammed closed, and Lisa tore into the room. I did not look up since this is the way Lisa usually enters the house and I was having trouble gluing the vertebrae. Suddenly, thrust between my nose and the half-glued tyrannosaur was Lisa's hand clutching a large black starling in what looked to me like the last throes of life. Its body was rigid, its beak was wide open (as though it were expecting a dentist to examine its teeth), its eyes bulged. "It's dying, it's dying, we've got to save it!" Without waiting for help, Lisa rushed off to show her dad. She reappeared a few minutes later with the bird. It now had a name, Trixie, and was housed in the cat carrier with all the comforts of home. It lay on a lavender hand towel next to a bowl of water and a bowl of puréed peanuts, which a visiting friend had ground up in the Cuisinart.

Lisa rinsed out the dropper from Schultz Liquid Plant Food and squeezed drops of water into Trixie's mouth. Trixie did not respond, and Lisa became hysterical—more hysterical than she had been the last time she tried to save a helpless creature, a bee floating in our neighbor's swimming pool. (I remember her running into the house crying, "We've got to save the bee!") In tears, Lisa begged me to take Trixie to the vet. I reached into the carrier, and, with my index finger on the top of its beak and my thumb on the bottom, squeezed Trixie's beak closed. It snapped back open. "Okay," I said, and Lisa (carrying the cat carrier containing Trixie), Alex, and I got into the car.

I was embarrassed to appear at the vet's with a dying starling. Let me amend that. I was embarrassed to appear at the vet's and announce that we had a life-and-death situation on our hands, insist that we be treated immediately, and then produce a dying starling—all of which I had to do to satisfy Lisa. After all, a starling is not a parrot or even a sparrow. And while I believe that no human being is better than another by virtue of birth, wealth, feathers, or whatever, I do not feel this way about birds. I do not think a starling should go to the vet at all. But if it does, it should wait its turn regardless of the circumstances. Everyone at the animal hospital, however, acted as if our urgency were perfectly understandable. Lisa and Alex had a crowd around them. Lisa had opened the cat carrier and was showing off Trixie, insisting that no one was allowed to touch her.

We were ushered into an examining room. The "nurse" (I am not sure what a person in this capacity at an animal hospital is called) picked up Trixie, who appeared to be in some bird death rattle, and left the room. I sat down to fill out a form on Trixie's vital statistics, none of which I knew, and sign an agreement to be responsible for the

medical costs. I didn't mind the cost but I was still re-
covering from the last time I had filled out one of these
forms. I had taken my cat, Pickles (also named by Lisa),
to the vet, and when they gave me his medicine, the tube
was labeled FOR PICKLES EPHRON.

As I was considering how I liked the sound of Trixie
Ephron, the nurse returned empty-handed and said she
was sorry but the bird was dead.

"Dead!" Lisa was furious. "Why? How?" Her hands
were on her hips. She seemed sure the nurse either was
lying or had done away with Trixie. "He swallowed poison," said the nurse. She then went into a long explanation
of how birds sometimes eat garden poisons intended for
insects. Lisa interrupted, "I want to see her."

"Would you please bring the bird back?" I said.

The nurse brought in Trixie, who looked exactly the
same in death as he (or she) had in life—body rigid, beak
now stuck permanently wide open, eyes bulging. "I can't
see," said Alex. I lifted him up so he could get a better
view. "I want to take Trixie home," said Lisa.

I was resigned. I had read enough child psychology
books to know this was something Lisa had to do.

The nurse put Trixie back in the cat carrier with the
water and puréed peanuts. Lisa locked the carrier and
picked it up. "Poison!" she said disgustedly as she left
the examining room. "Poison!" More outraged and in-
credulous, she marched through the waiting room to the

door. Suddenly, she stopped and looked at Alex.

"You swallowed a marble and you didn't die. Why didn't you die? Huh?" To me, enraged: "Why didn't Alex die? He swallowed a whole marble!"

On the way home, while Alex tried to poke the dead bird through the holes in the cat carrier, Lisa railed at him for not dying. "Why didn't you die? You swallowed a marble!" she kept saying. I didn't say anything. I was shocked into silence by the sudden collision of the two events. Lisa's fury, of course, was logical. She'd been let down two weeks in a row—Alex lived, Trixie died. These are bad breaks for an older sister. But listening to such a bald expression of sibling rage was unnerving. Yell at him when he gets to sit in the front seat or when he gets the first slice of cake, I thought, but don't get to the heart of the matter.

By the time we pulled into the driveway, Lisa had calmed down and was attacking Alex more conventionally. "Not only doesn't he die, but he doesn't cry!" she announced as though the two were equivalent. "Not about Trixie, not ever!" She slammed the car door and informed him, "A koala bear could fall out of a tree and land right in front of you, and would you cry? No!" Alex likes to please his sister—to the point of insisting that a marble is stuck in his throat (though not to the point of dying). He began to whimper, presumably for the loss of Trixie, but the effort was halfhearted.

Lisa lugged the cat carrier back into the house. Tearfully she showed her father the dead bird. Then she wrapped it in cotton, dug a grave (inadvertently uprooting the nasturtiums), and buried it. Two weeks later I went outside to check on our tomato plants and found Lisa and Alex digging up Trixie. "We want to see what she looks like now," said Lisa.

Car Talk

I back the car out of the driveway and head down the block.

"Oooooo, look at those guys."

"Foxyyyyy!"

The two twelve-year-olds are in the back seat. This is the way we always ride. Lisa and her friend Kim in the back, me in the front. Them talking, me listening.

"If you had all the children you could have from now until you couldn't have any more, you'd have forty children."

"Every year?"

"No! Altogether."

"Wow, think of all the Christmas presents you'd have to buy."

I never correct their inaccuracies. I suppose I could

say, "Girls, the maximum number of children a woman can have varies from woman to woman," and leave it at that. But even if I could bring myself to speak that sentence, setting them straight on the facts of life, even a fact as silly as this, is an exercise in futility. No sooner do you do it than they mix up what they are told with what they fear, hope, or imagine. The real choice a parent has is this: Do you tell a child the facts and then watch her make hash of them, or do you let her get an already cockeyed version from her friends? Either way, the result is the same.

So I stay out of it. Besides, if I say something—anything—Lisa and Kim might realize I'm listening. And they might stop talking. I make a right turn onto Wilshire Boulevard.

"Michael Jackson doesn't take female hormones anymore. Now he takes pills—steroids. But that's all. He doesn't drink, take drugs, or smoke."

"Thank God. I'd die if he smoked. I'd absolutely die."

"He's not gay anymore either."

"I know. He stopped when he was fourteen."

"Yeah, but the thing is, he tried to kill himself. He slit his wrists 'cause he found out his father's gay."

Lisa: *"That is dumb. Look, I love my dad. Nobody knows how much I love my dad. But I wouldn't slit my wrists if he were gay."*

"Yeah, but Michael Jackson's dad started him in show business."

I do not dwell on the logic of this. I do not dwell on the fact that this information (and almost all the information these girls exchange) sounds like it came from the *National Enquirer*. I find their conversation about Michael Jackson comforting, confirming my stepdaughter's stability. Think of it—my stepdaughter is too sensible to commit suicide if her father were homosexual. Never mind that it's my husband she's talking about. Never mind that it's a sensibleness of a limited sort. With any child entering adolescence, one hunts for signs of health, is desperate for the smallest indication that the child's problems will never be important enough for a television movie. I want to believe that, of course, I will be driven crazy when Lisa is a teenager, but only in a cute way.

So I rejoice in Lisa's practicality as I pull into the left lane and pass a car going too slowly.

"Kim, you know that guy I was going with, Robert?"

"Yeah."

"He was arrested for attempted murder."

"What?" I scream.

Lisa: "Delia, just forget I mentioned it. Forget it, okay?"

I slam on the brakes, realizing in the nick of time that the car in front of me has stopped for a light.

"Who is Robert?"

Lisa sighs. "He's this guy who lives in Ashley's building."

"I don't want you to speak to him again."

"It wasn't murder—it was just attempted murder."

"Lisa!"

Lisa sighs again.

"Now tell me exactly what happened."

"Well, Robert—he was really nice, too—got into a fight with an old lady and took a twenty-two and shot through her window."

"Is this the truth?"

"Ashley says so. Ashley never lies."

"Lisa, listen. If you know anyone who does anything criminal like that, you do not speak to him again. Ever! Do you understand? I don't want you hanging around with anyone who's violent."

"Duh," says Lisa.

Duh? I ignore the charm of this response. I suddenly feel ridiculous. Somehow sucked in. I remember that Ashley is also twelve. We ride in silence for a few blocks. Then:

Lisa, very excited: "Kim, let's say I was walking down the street and I saw Robert, okay. I wouldn't look at him. I'd just pretend I didn't see him and hold my head kinda sideways."

"Oooooo, neat," says Kim.

Girls, I want to scream, this is real life! But I don't. I shut up. It serves me right for listening. If you listen, you might hear. If you hear, you might mix up what they say with what you fear or imagine. It's a lot smarter and safer, if you want the news, to buy the *Enquirer*.

We are now five blocks from the department store. I move into the left lane to get there faster.

"Remember Vincent, the boy I got married to in recess in the fourth grade?"

I start humming. That's what I always did at the movies when I was a child. To block the sound, I hummed during the scary parts.

Mom in Love

Dear Diary,

You would not believe my algebra teacher, Mr. Brickley. His hair sits on top of his head like a bushel. Every time he says something, he writes it on the blackboard. I'm not kidding. Like if he says, "There will be a test Monday," he turns and writes "Monday" on the board. Also, he wears short-sleeved shirts and the flab on his arm waves when he writes. Oops— the phone.

It was for Mom—a guy. I hope he's better than the hypnotist she brought home from the Sierra Club. Maybe Mom should

marry Mr. Brickley. What a totally nau-
seous idea. Personally I am saving myself
for Sting.

9/15
Coffee with Sosa. Believes getting a Marx-
ist in dept. is essen.
Pro
    Is our only sig. gap in Euro. field.
    Am. hists. will secure app't. if we don't.
Con
    Fritz covers the field adequately.
    As regards Am. hists., so what?
Met a woman. A therapist.

DD,
    I just finished talking to Kristy on the
phone for three hours. A total and complete record. She says that Mr. Brickley
never writes his first name. He just puts M.
Mr. M. Brickley. Do you believe that? I
think the M stands for Moss! Wouldn't that
be a riot. Kristy looked "moss" up in the
dictionary and it said, "A spongy bog."
That is Mr. Brickley to a T.
    Poor Mom. She had this date tonight
and she couldn't decide what to wear. It
really cracked me up. She put on this dress

14

and it's like, How do I look? So I go,
"Okay." I really didn't want to tell her but
nobody wears dresses like that anymore.
But anyway she got it 'cause then she put
on these pants, which were a lot better,
and I loaned her my Guess shirt. But then
I just had to say something. "I can't believe
you're wearing those shoes." So she
changed them.

I just sat there watching her run around
deciding what to wear and cracking up. My
mom's kinda cute sometimes. I guess 'cause
she's a therapist and always thinking what
everything means, she goes into a spaz
when she has to look good. So then this
guy arrives. Joel. I couldn't believe it. He
was so little and round. She went to all that
trouble for a little round guy. I just said
hello and got out of there fast. Once she
wasn't ready and this guy kept saying things
to me like, "What are you studying?" So
lame.

9/30
Cooked dinner for Anne. Osso buco. Told
her about Scotty—he changed his major
for 3rd time. A. said: Can't be easy for him
to have mother who's Scientologist; father

15

who's medvl. hist. Found myself trying to
explain why married to L. 13 yrs. when
knew all along was wrong person. A. said I
probably didn't think I deserved it—love
and hap., that is.

A. very different from L. A Ph.D. in
clinical psych., a successful practice, a 14-
year-old dgtr. she's close to. A. said, unlike
L. she's "terrific" to be divorced from (i.e.,
doesn't take alimony). Ironic sense of
humor. Warm. Said her prob. with ex
was—cd. never tell him what she thought.
Hard to believe. Apparently has changed a
lot.

Heavy wk. Quartet rehearsal. Drinks
with Heller—Sosa wants me to lobby him.

A. said she'd never seen a kitchen as
org. as mine. Hope wasn't a criticism.

10/3
Stopped by Anne's today on spur of moment. Unlike me. Went bowling, which I
haven't done since age 10. Worried about
scoring lower than she. Am I doomed to
spend life worrying about lack of athletic
ability? Shades of h.s. Ridiculous. We took
Anne's dgtr. Jenny with us. Every time her
mother bowled, Jenny said, "Oh, Mom," as

if it were the most embarrassing moment
of her life. Seems sweet. Also shy.
Couldn't even get her to let me buy her a
Coke. It's funny—I even like it that Anne
has a dgtr.
    Started a diet today. Didn't plan to.
Found myself refusing dessert.

DD,
    I know you'll think I'm crazy but I think
Mom actually likes that butterball. I was
talking to Kristy about it and she said, "No
way," but I don't know. He stopped over
the other day without calling—I really
don't think Mom should put up with that—
and we all went bowling. I was really embarrassed for them that they wanted to go
bowling, and Mom kept saying that she
once bowled 150 when she was fifteen. I
mean, really, who cares? But anyway, she
kept giggling all the time and dropped the
bowling ball on her foot and the butterball
was rubbing it. It made me sick but she
liked it.
    I sorta miss my dad tonight.

DD,
    Right in the middle of Kristy and me

making up a song, "One Great Moss,"
Mom burst in spazzed because I forgot to
tell her Joel called. I don't see why she was
upset. It's not my fault I forgot.

10/11
Difficult day. Anne didn't return my call.
Suddenly thought it was over. A realiza-
tion: I couldn't imagine life going back to
what it was before Anne. Turned out Jenny
was busy and forgot to tell her I called.
   Told Sosa I don't give a shit about this
Marxist thing.

10/12
Quiet dinner with Anne. She pointed out
how much I tend to isolate myself. Might
even have picked medvl. hist. as profession
because it is cerebral and, for most peop.,
inaccessible.

10/15
Anne's in love with me. I am flying.

DD,
   Mom's really furious with me but I don't
care. Butterball was over again!!!!!!!!!!! and
I didn't say hello. Just 'cause someone says

hello to you doesn't mean you have to answer. Why should I be having these fake
conversations if I don't want to.

The main problem with Joel is he's always being so nice. And he's soooooooo
nosy!!!!!!!!!! He just comes into my room
and goes hi. Do you believe that? He
brought me one of Sting's albums. He said
he heard I liked him. I suppose *Mom* told
him. If she talks to him about me, I'll
never forgive her. Dad would never discuss
me with some strange person. Anyway, so
then I'm supposed to say thank you for
something I don't even want.

10/25
Seems Jenny's reacting a little to the fact
there's a man in her mother's life. Last
night I brought Anne a pint of her favorite
tofutti and I brought a Sting album for
Jenny. Jenny wouldn't say hello. In general
she hasn't been too friendly lately. Usually
I arrive and she retreats to her room. But
this time I went into her room to give her
the present. She wouldn't look at me. Lit-
erally refused to meet my eye. Anne suggested she say thanks. She did. To be
precise she said, "Thanks. Now can I go

back to what I was doing?" Anne was
pretty upset about it. Actually I find the
whole thing amusing. She's just a kid. It'll
pass.

DD,
   Something really terrible happened
today, diary. I came home from school and
opened the freezer and there was tofutti
there. Ever since it's been just Mom and
me, since I was five, Mom always made this
big deal—we should never have ice cream
in the house 'cause it was sugar and fatten-
ing. If you wanted ice cream, Mom said
you should just go out and buy one scoop
for a treat. I've always eaten junk at my
dad's and good food at my mom's. That's
the way it's always been. And now Joel's
bringing in mountains of tofutti like it's a
normal thing to do so they can eat it together.
   You know what I hate the most? When I
can hear them laughing.

   11/15
   Difficult that Anne leaves at 3 A.M. to go
   home. Said I'd be happy to stay at her
   place. (Surprised to hear myself say that.)

Anne doesn't want to upset Jenny more—
amazing, but in 9 yrs. Anne's never let a
man sleep over. Told her I'm not *any* man.
Anne said she'd think about it. Am so
crazy about her.

DD,
    Last night I slept over at Kristy's and I
got the feeling Mom was really happy I
did.

DD,
    Mom and Joel are having problems.
They spent all day sitting out in back talk-
ing about their relationship like total geeks.
Talk, talk, talk, talk, talk. I feel sorry for
Joel for falling in love with a therapist.
Maybe he'll realize what a mistake he's
made.

11/20
Told Anne she has to let me into her life
completely. I can't be in halfway. We're
acting like teenagers sneaking behind Jenny's back. A couple of nights ago, Jenny
slept over at a friend's and I felt as if it
were the warden's night off.
    Anne and I spent the day going over and

21

over it. She says she feels caught between
me and Jenny. I told her I'd do anything
for Jenny—I'm buying the whole package,
not just Anne. I'm sure Jenny's a lovely kid
when she isn't around me. I've always
wanted a daughter. Told Anne to trust
me—she said she's always had a problem
with that. I know Jenny's being difficult but
I can handle her.

11/26
That kid's a monster. I arrived for Thanksgiving, and walked into the room where
she was watching television, and said,
"Hello. What are you watching?" Nothing.
I might as well have been invisible. So I
said, "Oh, really. That sounds like a good
show," just to tease her, and she turned the
TV off, walked out, went into her room,
and slammed the door. Wouldn't come out
to eat.
    Anne was furious. She went in to talk to
Jenny and came out very upset.

DD,
    Thanksgiving was disgusting. If Mom
wants to invite Joel, fine, that's her decision. That doesn't mean I have to be with

him. I told her I thought on holidays you
were only supposed to invite people you
really cared about. Mom asked what I have
against him. I swear it is not personal. Totally objectively I really don't know what
she sees in him. I know he's a professor
but big deal. Medieval history is a dumb
thing to be a professor of. I told her I
didn't want to hurt her feelings but I don't
think he's good enough for her. She said I
should give him a chance. Actually what
she said, which was really, really disgusting,
was, "Jenny, I think you should try to open
your heart to him." I asked her if she ever
listens to the noise he makes when he
chews.

Mom would be better off with Mr.
Brickley. Maybe even a lot better off,
which is totally depressing if you think
about it.

P.S. I'm so glad I'm spending Christmas
vacation with my dad!

P.P.S. Maybe I shouldn't leave Mom and
Joel alone?

12/15
The monster leaves in three days. Thank
God.

DD,

If I don't talk to you before, Merry Christmas!!!!! And pray Mom and butter-ball break up for New Year's.

DD,

Do you believe this? On my first night home, Mom tells me butterball is moving in. We were at a restaurant having tacos and she told me. IN PUBLIC! How could she do that? I would never say something like that to her in public. That is so insensitive. I will never forgive her. And on my first night, too. She didn't even have the decency to wait a night. She thinks she's a shrink but she doesn't even know how to do anything. I asked her why she and Joel couldn't wait to live together till I'm out of high school. Then I'll be gone. She said it was too long. It's only three and a half years.

I think she's being desperate. She couldn't possibly love him. Mom says she knows it's hard for me. She said, "Jenny, change is scary." Well, she doesn't know. She doesn't know anything.

Joel is disturbing my entire life. I do not see why he doesn't see that Mom and I do

not need him. There is no room for him at
our house, and I don't know why he
doesn't get it.

DD,
   What I want to know is, what about his
stuff? Where's he going to put it? He has
this dog. And, diary, I haven't told you
'cause I didn't want to upset you, but he
has this son! He's twenty (and fat!) and he
lives in Chicago, but suppose he changes
his mind and moves here!!!!!!????
   I don't think Mom understands. This is
my house. Just point to a spot, diary, any
spot, and I can tell you everything about it.
This house is not supposed to be for more
people. Where will I fit??????????

1/10
Anne's furniture modern; mine mostly an-
tiques. Will they go together? I expressed
this concern to Anne, who said I was probably worried about how she, Jenny, and I
would go together, as opposed to the furniture. It's very comforting being in love
with a therapist—she always tells you what
you really mean. I think Anne's most worried about how neat I am, though she

hasn't said it. Anne, for instance, throws all
the utensils in a drawer. She does not use a
plastic separator.

DD,
   He's coming, diary, and I don't want
him. I want my mom! I want my whole
mom!!!!!!!!

DD,
   I gave Mom a list. He is not kissing me
good night, ever. I want my mom to come
into my room alone and do it. He is never
calling me Jennikins. That is Mom's name
for me and no one else's. He is not allowed
to use my telephone. He is not coming to
my school play. There is no way he is
going to see me play Calpurnia in *Julius
Caesar*.

DD,
   Joel is even weirder than I thought. His
furniture is about 400 years old. Mom and
I like new stuff. I knew he didn't belong
here. Maybe after she lives with one of his
ugly wood tables for a while, she'll realize
what a mistake she's made. Also, he puts
everything in jars. I mean he puts noodles

in jars and raisins and rice. Everything! He
opens all the cereal and mixes it together
in a jar. I do not like my cereal mixed up.
One thing's for sure, Sting would never do
that. Anyway, every time I pass a jar,
which is practically every second, I just un-
screw the top and take it off.

2/9

I put the top on a canister. The monster
takes it off. I think she actually bumps into
my coffee table on purpose. She's given
her mother a list. I am not allowed to kiss
her good night. I am not allowed to use
her telephone—this is something I'm
very interested in doing, of course. I am
not allowed to call her Jennikins. She
should know what I call her. I am not
allowed to see her play Calpurnia in *Julius
Caesar*. All very funny if it weren't infuriating.

I really don't know why she hates me.

2/14

I think I hate her! Now every time I say
something she waits two minutes and says,
"Excuse me, what did you say?" She's 14
years old, how can I hate her??????? How

27

can I hate Anne's daughter!!!!!!! Oh,
Christ. I certainly can't discuss this with
Anne.

DD,
   Either I'm moving in with Dad or I'm
moving in with Kristy. I've got to do something. I feel so out of it. Tonight Mom
came home from work really upset and was
talking to Joel about something that happened at the clinic. She used to talk to me
about those things. (Also, I don't really
think he gives the best advice.) What I feel
like has happened is before Joel I was not a
kid to Mom but I wasn't exactly an adult
either. Now he's here and I'm knocked
down a peg.
   Sometimes when they're in their room, I
think they're talking about me. I bet
they're plotting to get rid of me. Then they
can live happily ever after.

   3/1
   Happily ever after was invented by someone who did not have a stepchild.

DD,
   Here's what happened tonight. Mom

wanted chicken for dinner and I'm thinking
of becoming a vegetarian. So I was saying
that I really didn't want to eat what she was
making. So then Joel butted in and said,
"I'm sure we can have a compromise here."
That was so dumb. I just screamed at him,
"KEEP OUT OF IT!" If I am arguing with
my mom then I'm arguing with my mom. I
stomped out to call Kristy and heard him
say, "What's wrong with her now?" I
yelled, "Don't talk about me!"

Then Joel came downstairs and said, "I
need to talk to you." I just screamed, "I
hate you!" So then he put on this sad face
which made me even madder. "Look
Jenny," he said, "it hurts me when you talk
to me like that."

"Well, how do you think I feel? You're
ruining my life."

"I don't want to ruin your life."

"Ha."

Then he said, what nerve, "Jenny, I
know you have a really special relationship
with your mom and I don't want to interfere. I've never had a daughter—"

"I'm not your daughter!!!!!!!!!!!!!!" I
knew that's what he wanted, diary, I
knew it!!!!!!!!!!!!

3/6
Still can't figure out what happened. Jenny
suddenly decided to become a vegetarian,
and Anne had been planning to cook
chicken. I suggested we compromise. Jenny
blew up and stormed out.

I went in to talk to her. She was screaming she hates me, she's not my daughter. I
was just trying to tell her I was sorry she
was so upset. I've never had a daughter so
I might make mistakes sometimes. I don't
know why I wanted to tell her that. I don't
know why I was being nice. She's a pain in
the ass and I'm sick of her. Why does she
exist? I had to go out for an hour to calm
down.

Anne's beside herself. How could her
happiness be causing her daughter this
much pain? She said, in a way, it's her
fault. By not being with a man all these
years, she's led Jenny to believe there
would never be anyone but the two of
them. Anne also thinks Jenny is protecting
her father. Apparently he hates to buy anything that isn't on sale and it makes Jenny
worry about him.

Anne thinks if only Jenny would let herself, she could get so much from me. (It

was sweet of her to say that.) Anyway,
we've made a pact. We're going to stop discussing Jenny.

DD,

Mom thinks I should see a shrink. I AM
NOT SEEING A SHRINK. In my opinion
the only reason shrinks have business is
that other shrinks send them their kids.
Mom said, "You're obviously feeling a lot
of upsetting things. I know my being with
Joel has been very difficult for you." At
least she's right about that. I asked her if
she was going to forget my birthday. She
said she thought I was really worried that
she was going to forget *me*. It drives me
crazy that she's always telling me what I
really mean. But then, you know what,
diary? She started crying. "Couldn't you try
to like Joel a little? He's so nice." Maybe
I've hurt her. Maybe she's crying like crazy
right now. Good.

Last night I had a dream that I found
Joel kissing someone else and poor Mom
was so upset, I had to kick him out.

3/15
A splitting headache. Told Anne I didn't

think she should allow Jenny to mistreat me. A. said I was the adult, Jenny the child, I should handle it—can't make her choose between us. Told her I was not making her choose. I simply thought she should be stricter with Jenny. "Don't tell me how to raise Jenny!"

"I live here too."

"She's not your child."

"Oh, I get it. First I'm supposed to handle it; now I'm not supposed to handle it. If I can't discipline her, you do it. You're not strict enough."

"Don't judge me."

"I'm not judging you!"

"You're watching how I treat Jenny and judging it. I can't have you watching me all the time."

"Me watching you? That's a joke, coming from a shrink. You're the one who's always telling everyone what they mean. I can't live here if I have nothing to say about your daughter."

"Fine, don't live here. We were fine before you came, and we'll be fine after you leave."

"Fine."

3/16

Anne and I have decided to get married.

3/24

Set the date for May 21 and found myself
pouring lentils into my cereal bowl this
morning. Jenny pointed out, if I didn't put
things in jars, that wouldn't have happened.
I guess with Jenny around, I'll never be too
far from reality.

4/4

Anne says she's sure getting married is a
character flaw. (I'm glad she's flawed.) She
can't think of a reason why it makes sense.
She even suggested she's getting married
because she likes to keep up with trends
and getting married is now fashionable. She
was kidding, of course. I know this sounds
odd but the reason I want to get married
is, when we're dead, I want it to be that
husband and wife was what we were to
each other. Is that morbid or romantic?
Anne says it's appropriately medieval.
Jenny said, yuck.

DD,

I know I haven't written for a while

'cause I've been major depressed. Tomorrow Mom and butterball are getting married, only he's not a butterball anymore
'cause he's lost some weight. Kristy calls
him dietball. Anyway Mom bought this
white dress—it's not long but it's so inappropriate. I'm really embarrassed for her.
I'm supposed to be in the wedding, but
maybe I'll get paralyzed tomorrow and not
be able to get out of bed.

Suppose I have to take Joel's last name?
I asked my dad. He said no one could ever
change my name, but suppose they make a
special case? I bet Dad's really upset but
not showing it. I bet he's a wreck. I swear
the word stepfather will never cross my
lips. I'll call Joel stepshit.

P.S. His son is here and fatter than his
picture! Butterball II.

5/20
No wedding bells but we'll have quartet
music in our living room. Actually it will
be a trio since they'll have to do without
yours truly. Anne's childhood friend who's
a defrocked priest will perform the ceremony, and the university chaplain will sign

the license. Jenny has had the decency to
suffer quietly. Told Anne I really appreci-
ate that. There is one hopeful sign. Jenny's
stopped taking the tops off canisters.

I sat Jenny down tonight and told her I
had no intention of trying to take her father's place. I know she has a father. I
hope she heard me.

DD,

The wedding was awful. Mom was just
glowing all the time and Joel was racing
around trying to make everyone comfortable as usual. Kristy came and we made this
pact. After they got married, we kept hugging each other over and over so no one
would notice I wasn't hugging Joel, especially Joel. But then he asked me to dance.
I had to dance with him 'cause it was his
wedding, but I just looked down all the
time. People were taking pictures. I wanted
to die.

Kristy has decided that her plan for this
summer is to get a boyfriend. So we went
to get T-shirts with our phone numbers
printed on them. It was so hysterical. She
did it but I was too embarrassed. I put my
zip code on instead.

DD,

Joel bought me a helmet to wear when I bike-ride. At first I couldn't decide whether to buy this purple helmet with silver flecks on it even though I loved it, 'cause the color didn't exactly go with my bike. Also I might look weird riding down the block with purple on my head. But Joel said, "Go for it."

P.S. I was really surprised when Joel said, "Go for it." He never seemed like the type.

6/3

Jenny hugged me.

DD,

Tonight was dress rehearsal for *Julius Caesar*. Mom helped me make my toga out of a bed sheet. It kept falling off till Mom fastened it with about fifty safety pins. She swears it will stay up.

Mom and Joel are going AND my dad is flying in. That should be strange. Suppose I have to introduce Joel? "Uh, Dad, this is the man my mom married." Get me out of here! Kristy is stage manager and she

swears that if my toga falls down, she'll
drop the curtain.

6/8
Heller wanted to know if I was going to
teach Thomas à Becket again next fall. Said
yes even though I'll probably have six students. Am beginning to accept that what I
like is never going to be fashionable.
    Met Anne's ex. He looks older for his
age than I do for mine.

DD,
    The play was so incredible, diary, but
you wouldn't believe it. Moss Brickley was
there with his wife, and if you saw her,
you'd faint. Oh, rats, gotta go. Mom and
Joel are taking me out for pizza, then I'm
sleeping at Kristy's with Debra, who's becoming my second-best friend. Ta, ta, as
they say in Rome.

Phone Calls

"Hi, Josh, it's Daddy. How are you?"
"Fine."
"How was school?"
"Fine."
"Wha'd you learn today?"
"Nothing."
"Nothing? Well, what did you do after school?"
"Nothing."
"Didn't you go to Rebecca's birthday party?"
"Oh, yeah."
"Was it fun?"
"What, Dad?"
"I said, 'Was it fun?'"
"What?"

"Rebecca's birthday. What are you doing? Are you watching TV?"

"Yeah."

"Mom lets you watch in the afternoon? She didn't used to."

"Huh?"

"I said, what show are you watching?"

. . . "What, Dad?"

"Never mind. Listen, I'll call you back later."

"Okay. 'Bye, Daddy."

"Hi, Josh, it's Daddy. What are you doing?"

"I'm playing with Ricky."

"What are you playing?"

"Hello."

"Who is this? Oh, Ricky."

"Is this Josh's dad?"

"Yes. Would you put Josh back on?"

"Hi, Dad, that was Ricky. He wanted to say hello."

"Listen, I'll call you back when you're not playing."

"Okay. 'Bye, Daddy."

"Hi, Josh, it's Daddy."

"Hi, Daddy, guess what? I just got back from the movies. Mom took me."

"Wha'd you see?"

39

"Oh, Dad, it was so funny. It was about this robot, but he wasn't really a robot. I mean on his planet he was a regular, but here he was a robot."

"Yeah."

"And his hands had these things inside so they could shoot like pistols, but he didn't want to shoot them—oh, but I forgot to tell you that before, the robot loved hot dogs, but he got all mixed up and put a French fry in a bun."

"Yeah."

"And he went into a banana truck 'cause there was this car chase."

"Yeah."

"Only the robot wasn't in a car 'cause he had his own wheels but not an engine, so he was only sort of a car but he could go as fast as one. And he went by these people and their coffee fell over. It was so funny. Wanna go? And then you know what? A man took the robot's place but they were . . . oh, neat!"

"What? . . . Josh? Josh, what's going on? What's that music? What are you doing? Josh, pick up the phone."

"That was Duran Duran on the radio. Wanna hear some more?"

"No. Forget it. I'll call you back later."

"Okay. 'Bye, Daddy."

"Hi, Daddy, it's Josh."

"Hi. What's happening?"

"Mom bought me a new pair of sneakers."

"Hey, that's great. What color?"

"I don't want to! I don't want to! I'm talking to my dad!!! . . . Dad, Mom says I have to clean up my room now, hold on."

"Hold on? I can't hold on while you clean up your room. That's ridiculous. Josh? Are you there? Josh, pick up the phone. Josh?"

"Hi, it's me. Can I speak to Josh?"

"He's eating dinner right now."

"Okay, I'll call back later."

"Hi. Can I speak to Josh now?"

"He's going to sleep."

"Just put him on for a second, okay?"

"This is not a good time."

"I just want to say good night to my son."

"If he talks to you, he'll get all excited."

"So what?"

"So then I'm stuck with a hyped-up kid who can't fall asleep."

. . . "Just tell him I called."

The Toy

The Jump-O-Leen was a present to Lisa on her eighth birthday and she loved it, which was why we found it in the car as we were about to leave for the beach. The Jump-O-Leen, a poor man's trampoline, is a large black inner tube with one side covered by heavy orange plastic. In the back seat of our car, it took up about four-fifths of the space and entirely obscured the view out the rear window.

"This is out of the question," said Lisa's father, removing the Jump-O-Leen. Lisa begged—she couldn't leave without it. Larry relented, but insisted it could not ride inside the car. Over her protests, he fastened it to the roof rack with six pieces of elasticized rope. Lisa and her younger brother, Alex, climbed up on the hood to check his work. "It will fall off," said Lisa.

We got into the car and headed for Trancas, a Malibu beach, because Larry and I had a craving for buttermilk doughnuts, and we once ate great ones at a pastry shop in Trancas. We were on the Pacific Coast Highway, going about 50 miles an hour, when Lisa announced that something was wrong, she could hear the Jump-O-Leen "moving around."

"Lisa, the Jump-O-Leen's not moving around," I said. Then I heard a bump. I looked out the back window. The Jump-O-Leen had flown off the roof and was bouncing down the highway.

Lisa screamed. Alex started crying. Larry and I watched, terrified, as several cars behind us swerved, narrowly missing it and each other. The Jump-O-Leen careened along. Then, miraculously having caused no accident, it came to rest safe from the flow of traffic on the broken white line between lanes on our side of the highway.

"Turn around, Dad, turn around!" yelled Lisa. Alex stopped crying. Larry and I were whipping our heads backward and forward, torn between watching the Jump-O-Leen recede in the distance and looking for a place to make a turn. The highway was divided by a center platform, and there was no place to cut over to the other side of the road and head back. We sped up a hill, and, as we went over the crest, the Jump-O-Leen disappeared from sight.

Lisa burst into tears. "Stop it!" I said. I was furious—furious that she was carrying on like this, furious that we couldn't do anything about it.

We barreled along. My eyes were fixed on the farthest point in the road, searching for a break in the highway. The only sounds from the back seat were loud hiccuping noises, Lisa's way of informing us that, because she was not allowed to cry, she would choke on her tears instead. After what seemed like fifteen miles but was about two, we came to a break in the road. We made a U-turn and headed back.

Silent with anticipation, we came over the crest of the hill again. Way down the highway was a little orange dot. "It's still there!" cried Lisa. We raced down the hill. Of course, now we were on the wrong side of the divided road—we would have to pass the Jump-O-Leen, find a place to turn around, and come back to pick it up. But we could see it and were incredibly relieved. We also happened to notice a pickup truck that pulled over to the edge of the road next to the Jump-O-Leen. The driver, a teenage boy with shaggy brown hair, jumped out of the truck, ran into the road, picked up the Jump-O-Leen, and ran back. As we whizzed by, all four of us screaming across the divider, "Stop, that's our Jump-O-Leen," which the boy couldn't possibly hear, he tossed the Jump-O-Leen into the back of the truck, hopped in, and drove off.

44

Lisa wailed, "Catch him, Daddy. You've got to catch him." But now we had to drive a half-mile farther before we came to another break in the road. By the time we turned around, the pickup was out of sight.

"It's hopeless," said Larry. "I'm afraid we've lost the Jump-O-Leen."

Lisa burst into fresh, much worse tears. Larry said, "I know it's sad, but there's nothing we can do. I promise I'll buy you a new Jump-O-Leen."

"I don't want a new Jump-O-Leen. I want that Jump-O-Leen. It was my friend."

More sobs from the back as we passed the place in the road where the Jump-O-Leen had once lain. Lisa spotted a police car and suggested that if we told the policeman what had happened, he'd get our Jump-O-Leen back. Larry and I did not want to tell a policeman that a Jump-O-Leen had blown off our car in the middle of the Pacific Coast Highway. I couldn't even imagine saying the word "Jump-O-Leen" to a person outside the family.

Silence as we went over the crest of the hill, leaving the scene of the disaster. Then Alex: "It's your fault, Lisa. You shouldn't have brought it."

Lisa: "It is not! Dad, I told you it would fall off."

Larry: "It wasn't my idea to take the Jump-O-Leen to the beach."

I felt, but did not say, that a toy this ridiculous should never have been made, that Larry should have known not to put it on the roof, that Lisa should not have been so

45

determined to have her way. And I was pretending I felt none of these things because I couldn't help noticing how our family behaved in a crisis: we got mad at each other. This didn't seem right. "It's nobody's fault," I said loudly.

Twenty minutes later. We were almost to Trancas, Lisa still sniffling, when from a dirt road off the highway a pickup truck pulled out directly in front of us. Through the rear window of the truck, I saw shaggy brown hair.

"Dad, that's it! That's the truck! Stop him!" yelled Lisa.

"It is," I said amazed.

Larry accelerated, switched into the next lane, and pulled up alongside the pickup. Lisa, Alex, and I waved frantically to get the driver's attention. I rolled down the window.

"You have our Jump-O-Leen," I yelled. "And our little girl is upset. She loves that toy and we need it back."

I should just mention here that, in times of crisis, I often attempt to use psychology I have picked up from reading women's magazines. In this case, it was something obvious—if one helps an upset child articulate her feelings, she will experience less trauma. I was probably reading about what to do when a child loses a parent, not a toy. Nevertheless, this is the reason why, at 50 mph, I found myself making a speech about Lisa's attachment to her Jump-O-Leen. The words were actually directed at Lisa, but I figured the boy was more likely to return the Jump-O-Leen if he knew a child was suffering.

It seems absurd that this much calculation passed through

my mind between the time I rolled down the window and the time I yelled out of it, but it did. So here I was sounding like Eda LeShan when what I was really worried about was this boy might not have the vaguest idea what a Jump-O-Leen was and that the thing he'd picked up was one.

But the boy, who looked a little confused at the beginning, caught on and nodded in recognition. He pulled off onto the shoulder of the road. We pulled over behind him. He hopped out, got the Jump-O-Leen, and handed it over.

Larry stuck the Jump-O-Leen in the back with the kids. Lisa pulled it onto the seat beside her. It still took up about four-fifths of the space. Lisa and Alex were wedged between it and the door.

As we pulled out onto the highway, Lisa put her arms around the Jump-O-Leen as far as she could reach. "Who wants doughnuts?" said Larry.

"Me!" screamed Lisa and Alex.

"Me, too," I said. I couldn't help noticing how our family behaved when a crisis was over: we ate.

Three Parts,
Three Players

Scene i
Place: DADDY'S HOUSE
Time: SUNDAY NIGHT

DAD: You can't take that to your mother's.

ALLISON: Why?

DAD: It stays here. It belongs in this house. Every toy I get you ends up there, and then there's nothing here and there's nothing for you to play with.

ALLISON: Oh, Daddy, please, please. I love it so much. I'll bring it back, I really will.

DAD: Tell your mom to buy you one.

ALLISON: She won't. She never buys me anything.

DAD: Never?

ALLISON: Never.

DAD: Allison, I give your mother money every month to buy you things.

ALLISON: Everything she gets me is crummy.

DAD: Look, you and I both know that your mother has trouble spending money, but the toy stays here. I am sick and tired of having everything I get you disappear.

ALLISON: I'll bring it back, I really will. Please, please, please.

DAD: If you don't, I will never buy you anything again. Ever. Do you understand?

ALLISON: Oh, thanks, Daddy, thanks. I love you so much. I love you, I love you, I love you.

Scene 2
Place: MOMMY'S HOUSE
Time: 20 MINUTES LATER

ALLISON: Hey, Mom, look what Dad got me!

MOM: Another toy?

ALLISON: You know what we did? We went to Disney-land.

MOM: Again?

ALLISON: Yeah, and you know what we had for breakfast? Pop Tarts.

MOM: Pop Tarts before you went to Disneyland?

DAD: It was a special treat.

ALLISON: I stayed up until eleven o'clock.

MOM: Another special treat. Did you bring your socks back from Dad's? *(To her ex-husband)* All her socks are disappearing. *(To her daughter)* Aren't they, sweetie?

ALLISON: Hey, Dad, want to come in and see what I did to my room?

MOM: Not tonight, dear. Daddy will see it next time.

DAD: Mommy's right. It's late. Give me a kiss.

ALLISON: 'Bye, Daddy. I love you so much. I love you, I love you, I love you.

A Death in
the Divorced Family

He got the call at 8 A.M. "Is Amanda there?"

"No," said Jim.

"Good," said Barry. "Patsy died."

Amanda is an eleven-year-old girl. Barry is her step-father. She lives with him and her mother, Vanessa, who was away on a business trip, which is why Barry, not Vanessa, called Jim, her father, at whose apartment Amanda had slept the previous night, a Wednesday, the night she always spent with her father and the woman he lives with, Karen. But as it was 8 A.M., Amanda had already left for school. Patsy was her pet guinea pig.

Barry was calling to convey his and Vanessa's joint decision that Amanda should be told of Patsy's death after school and in person. Would Jim do it? He was her father.

He was also the only person among the four of them—
Vanessa, Barry, Jim, and Karen—who did not have a
nine-to-five job. Jim worked sporadically, which was normally a source of irritation to Vanessa and a continual
reminder that she was right to have divorced him: he
wasn't steady.

"For once his not working comes in handy," said Barry
over the phone to Vanessa, though all Barry said to Jim
was, "Vanessa wondered if you could meet Amanda after
school, break the news, and tell her not to open the
freezer compartment of the refrigerator because Patsy is
there."

Jim's first reaction to hearing of the death of a pet his
daughter had had for nine years was this: "Thank God
Patsy didn't die at my house, I would have been blamed."
He didn't say so to Barry, of course, but it was the first
thing he said to Karen when he called her at work to tell
her about Patsy. He and Karen agreed that Vanessa and
Barry were right for once—Amanda should be told in
person—but wasn't it typical of Vanessa to try to or-
chestrate everything, even Jim's behavior in regard to
Patsy's death?

Jim met Amanda after school. He then called Karen
to say that Amanda had not been particularly upset; as
usual, Vanessa had assumed Amanda would be trauma-
tized when she wasn't. He then called Barry to say Amanda
was fine and would stay out of the freezer. Barry called
Vanessa to tell her.

Vanessa and Barry then discussed the burial. They assumed Amanda would want Patsy buried at the house in the country, which Jim had kept in the divorce settlement but for which Amanda had always had a "special feeling" because she spent a month there every summer and had lived there before the divorce. So when Barry got home from work, he talked it over with Amanda and then called Vanessa back to tell her they had figured correctly. Then he called Jim but got his answering machine. Barry hung up thinking, Typical, he's never there when you need him. Jim called back an hour later and Barry told him about the burial and the problem it presented: He and Vanessa thought Patsy should be buried this weekend because they were not sure how long she would keep in the freezer, but it was not Jim's weekend to have Amanda; it was his and Vanessa's. So Vanessa and he wondered if Jim and Karen would go up to the country house without Amanda, but with Patsy, and bury her. Jim said he would check with Karen and call back.

Jim called Karen, who was working late, and they agreed to go. Karen hung up thinking that, even though she did not mind going to the country, she was sure Patsy would keep another week but no one ever really cared what she thought anyway. Furthermore, this was one more example of Vanessa's interfering in their life.

Just before Jim and Karen fell asleep that night, Jim started laughing. He said it was so typical of Vanessa to have Barry make all these telephone calls for her when she was out of town—she was too cheap even to call long distance. Karen said, "Isn't it funny? I was just thinking the same thing." Jim reminded Karen of the time he decided to send Amanda to camp and all Vanessa wanted to know was would he pay for it and was he going to deduct the cost from his child support?

The next evening, Amanda called her dad to say she wanted Patsy buried near the briar patch next to the path to the barn. Jim could hear Vanessa, now returned from her trip, coaching in the background, "Tell him to be sure to take this seriously." He hung up furious.

"This is one more instance of her not trusting me," he said to Karen. He told her about the time Vanessa went to London and arranged for Amanda to stay with her aunt instead of with him when he lived only six blocks from her school and the aunt lived twenty. At the same time, over a glass of wine, Vanessa was telling Barry that Jim never took anything seriously. Once he took Amanda hiking and she broke her ankle. Vanessa didn't even get a phone call. She just opened the door and there was Amanda with a cast on her leg. Vanessa paused, then said, "I wouldn't be surprised if Jim only pretended to bury Patsy."

Jim and Karen went to pick up Patsy on Friday afternoon. No one was home. Vanessa had left the key under a flowerpot. Jim found Patsy in the freezer, wrapped in plastic wrap and then in two plastic garbage bags. "If you ever needed proof of what an uptight guy Vanessa married, look at this," he said, showing the thrice-wrapped guinea pig to Karen. He then put Patsy in the trunk since it was winter and he was concerned that she might defrost if she were inside the car during the three-hour ride.

Jim and Karen buried Patsy in the spot Amanda had requested, though it was quite difficult because the ground had recently frozen. Jim made a joke about Vanessa's being somehow responsible for this. Then they went inside, built a fire, and had some wine. Jim reminisced about Amanda and Patsy: how sweet she kept the pet so long; how, when Amanda was five, Patsy would play with her in her wading pool; how Patsy ate raisin bran out of Amanda's hand; and how last year Vanessa tried to ruin it all—she insisted that Patsy was too old to run loose in the briar patch, even though Jim's ex-girlfriend, who was also named Karen, had kids who had old guinea pigs who ran loose in the briar patch. Jim tried to explain to Vanessa that all guinea pigs do is make tunnels, but Vanessa wouldn't change her mind. So rigid, so overprotective, so bossy. So typical.

Some Famous Couples
Discuss Their
Divorces

Dick & Jane

Jane
When Dick left me, I got depressed. I mean really depressed. But now I'm going to a therapist and it's been incredible. In my first session, he said, "What do you want?" It was so brilliant because you know what I realized? I didn't know! I mean it was always Dick and Jane, Dick and Jane, never just Jane. My shrink says I was intimidated by Dick. Like even though it was my money too, I never felt it was. When I bought a pair of shoes, I always told Dick the price minus two dollars so it wouldn't seem as much. I mean, even though it was Dick and Jane, it was like Dick was in capital letters and Jane was in

lower case. Also, though Dick denies it, he always acted as if what I said wasn't as important as what he said. If he said, "Look, look," I always looked. But if I said, "Look, look," he didn't pay any attention.

Spot is living with me and visits Dick on alternate weekends. I got the house and pretty much all the furnishings because Spot needs continuity.

Dick

It's true I was having an affair with Eloise, but I don't think she was the reason the marriage broke up per se. Jane and I never should have been married in the first place. We'd been going together since we were kids, and she said it wasn't going anywhere and we had to break up or get married. So we got married.

It's been rough being without Spot. What I miss most is the dailiness—the walks, the feedings. My watching the football game in one room, while Spot scratched himself in another. When we're together now, it seems like we're always doing things. I'm either throwing a ball or a bone. We never just hang out.

What makes it really hard is that Eloise's dog, Weenie, is living with us. I don't get to be Spot's master but I have to be stepmaster to Weenie. Luckily, when Spot visits, he and Weenie get along great. The problem is Eloise and I have different rules for raising dogs. She lets Weenie sleep at the bottom of our bed. Spot has always slept on the service porch. I can tell from how he whimpers at night he doesn't think it's fair that Weenie gets to be in the bedroom. Eloise says if she moves Weenie out of the bedroom now he'll feel rejected, and he's feeling insecure these days as it is. Well, so is Spot. I don't know. The only thing Eloise and I ever fight about is the dogs.

Minnie Mouse & Mickey Mouse

Minnie

I was the one who did it. I kicked him out. But he made my life so miserable I had to. That's always been Mickey's game—passive aggression. It really pisses me off. He acts like a bastard, then gets to be the victim.

What an infant! His priorities are completely screwed up. Like if I was about to be eaten by a cat and Mickey ran into a lost mouse, he'd spend an hour making sure the mouse got where he was supposed to, and to hell with me. Mickey's always wanted to be loved—by the masses, by the studio, by everyone but his wife. Well, he says I'm supposed to love him no matter what. I told him he's got me mixed up with his mother.

I gave up my career for Mickey. I was going to be just as famous as he, but, no, Mickey wanted me to stay home with the kids. The only time I had any fun was when the company trotted me out for a stockholders' meeting. And then they always wanted me to wear the same damn thing— a polka-dot dress and those ridiculous high heels. Do you

58

know what it feels like to wear shoes that are too large for you? Mickey couldn't stand it when I complained. He said he didn't mind the shorts with large buttons, why should I mind the polka dots and the shoes? Doesn't he realize he's just a figurehead, a glorified P.R. man? Maybe he does. Maybe he feels empty and that's why he screws anything that squeaks. Whatever. It's not my problem anymore.

It's really strange how everything changes. Mickey and I were together fifty years, and now when I see him, I think, Who is this mouse? How was I ever attracted to him?

Mickey
Everything I have to say about this I've already said through my agent.

Archie & Veronica

Archie
I guess I just don't get it. I always thought we were the perfect couple, but when I told Betty, Reggie, and Jughead that Veronica and I were splitting, they said they'd been expecting it for years. Veronica says we're just not in the same place anymore. She says we never really were, it just seemed like it because, in high school, we were both popular. Anyway, I'm holding her back. She says I

never take anything seriously, even California wines, and my idea of a good time is to go to a high school basketball game with the old crowd. I told her I'd change. I'll root for the NBA. She said, "Great," like really sarcastically. It seems like nothing's ever enough for her.

Betty's been really helpful through this, pointing out all the ways Veronica hasn't been there for me. Betty's a family therapist now so she knows a lot about this stuff. At first we just met for coffee and talked, ya know, kinda informally. But I'm going to have my first real session Saturday night. It's the only time she can see me.

Veronica

That was my best friend, Betty, on the phone. She has been so great to me through this you wouldn't believe it—calling every day. Friends are so important, aren't they? But it's really strange. Aren't you supposed to be depressed when you get divorced? I've never felt better. Because of this divorce, I've found a career. I'm going to be a consultant to divorcing couples on splitting up their belongings. Isn't that fantastic? I always knew Archie was holding me back, but until I got divorced, I never knew from what.

I made up all these rules. They worked so well for me and Archie that I just know they'll work for everyone else. For one thing, they're based on fairness. That's the most important part. Do you want to hear them? Great.

First of all, whatever you inherited, you keep. In the case of Archie and me, that meant I got the china, silver, flatware, and crystal. Anything that was your hobby, you also keep. Furnishing the house was my hobby, so I kept the house and the furniture. Archie kept his collection of high school yearbooks and his sixteen letter sweaters. If you both collected something together, you split the collection in half unless one of you put in much more time collecting than the other. Then that person gets more, proportionate to the amount of time put in. For example, since I was the one who was pregnant and gave birth, I got to pick two children for Archie's one. We have two kids so I kept them both. When I tried to discuss this with Archie so he would understand my reasoning, he said, "Do whatever you want." And that brings up another thing I discovered: In order for the splitting up of things to work, both people don't have to participate. The only thing Archie contributed was his saying that if one person made fun of an object, the other should get it. Well, fine, that's his loss because he thinks everything is a big joke and I have no sense of humor.

Wait, there's more. Anything that your parents paid for, you get. For instance, Daddykins gave us the money for the stereo and the car so I got them. Record collections should be divided in half—rock 'n' roll selected by performer, classical by composer. But—and here it gets a little complicated—if you have nothing on which to use something, then you don't get the thing because what would you do with it? So I ended up taking all the records because I had the stereo.

You see, it's important to be fair, but you must also be practical at the same time.

Nancy Drew & Ned Nickerson

Ned

Quite seriously, Nancy needs help, has for years. She's a workaholic. For the longest time, I just didn't realize it. Before we were married I thought she was so—I guess you'd say, cool. The other girls were boring debutantes, and Nancy was always disappearing in a rowboat with a foreigner named Romano. Of course, in those days her sleuthing was less frequent. She had about one mystery a year. But then all of a sudden she was up to one a month, then one a week. Sleuthing became compulsive. If the car wouldn't start, it became "The Clue in the Carburetor." If the refrigerator went on the blink, it became "The Secret of the Melting Ice." The maid quit, and it was "The Clorox Conspiracy." I tried to get her into a treatment program but she refused. In fact, she won't discuss her neurosis. She won't even admit her sleuthing *is* a neurosis. I think she has a problem expressing her feelings. That's fits, doesn't it? If you spend all day sleuthing, it's a way to avoid yourself.

I've done a considerable amount of reading now that I'm alone. *I'm OK—You're OK; Living, Loving, and Learning; When Bad Things Happen to Good People.* I don't think I was held enough as a child, and that's why I was attracted to someone cold and distant like Nancy. I'm working on hugs now and dating someone who's Jewish.

Nancy

I only have a minute because I'm working on "The Clue in the Out-of-Court Settlement." The problem with Ned and me in a nutshell: He's jealous. While we were going together he always acted as if he liked it that I sleuthed. We got married and overnight it was, "Can't you just sleuth part-time?"

What's really bothering me is that Ned thinks he's entitled to fifty percent of the proceeds from my books. Ned says if it weren't for him, I wouldn't have been as successful as I was. Having a boyfriend made me more appealing to the public, and if he hadn't been holding down the fort—providing me with a secure relationship to come home to—I couldn't have had all my adventures. That's easy for him to say. He's not the one who was kidnapped by a gypsy violinist or poisoned by a sword doll. Besides, I was always encouraging him to sleuth, but he didn't want to.

Daddy's handling the divorce for me. He says not to worry.

Olive Oyl & Popeye

Popeye

I hate to think of Swee'pea growing up with that woman as his mother (or should I say, as her mother? I've never been absolutely sure what sex Swee'pea is. I think a boy). Olive is a complete control freak. Just get a load of the poor kid's schedule. Monday, clarinet; Tuesday, computer class; Wednesday, soccer; Thursday, scouts; Friday, gymnastics. I don't think he has any fun when he's with her. And she's always acting like I'm not a responsible person. Just because I don't have a job. When I take Swee'pea sailing, she always says, "Don't forget to put sun block on him." She claims I once brought him back as red as a lobster, which isn't true. "Oh, Popeye," she shrieked. "Look what you've done!" Somebody should do something about that voice. I thought when we got married it would lower a few octaves, but I found out marriage doesn't change anything.

I think Swee'pea's going to want to live with me when he's older. I wish he did right now. If he's a boy, he'd be better off with his father.

Olive

Okay, so he rescued me a few times when we were younger.
Popeye always liked to put on a big show when everyone
was watching. Most of the time, he just lay around on
that boat with a pipe in his mouth. I suppose I shouldn't
complain. The truth is, I don't need him anymore because, now that I've taken karate, I can rescue myself.

Popeye's always been pretty good to Swee'pea considering we never did know who his father is and I'm not
sure I'm his mother. Though I wish Popeye would grow
up already. When I first met him, I thought it was so cute
the way he flipped the tops off tin cans and poured the
contents down his throat. We all did things like that when
we were kids. But now he's forty and it's time to use a
knife and fork. Popeye says I'm so uptight. Just because
Swee'pea has Monday, clarinet; Tuesday, computer class;
Wednesday, soccer; Thursday, scouts; Friday, gymnastics. I'm not uptight; he's irresponsible. Once he brought
Swee'pea back from sailing as red as a lobster. Men have
it so easy. Doesn't he realize what it's like being a single
mother? He takes Swee'pea out, buys him whatever he
wants, and drops him off. I'm the real parent—I'm the
one who makes sure he studies, gets enough sleep, and
talks to him about his feelings about androgyny. I guess
when it comes to Swee'pea, you could say that I'm the
lettuce, Popeye's the dressing, which is pretty ironic if
you think about it.

Snow White & the Prince

Snow White

Off the record, he's a pervert. He only wanted to do it if I was drugged. I had to take a 'lude, pass out, and then he'd wake me with a kiss. At first I thought it was sort of sweet—re-creating the first time we met and all. But then it turned out, if I wasn't unconscious, he couldn't get it up. That's sick. It's only logical I began to look for comfort elsewhere. What would you expect?

To be honest, I suppose it was inevitable. There was always this unresolved thing between me and Doc (he's so take-charge), and me and Bashful (secretly he's a tiger), and me and Happy (such a compelling laugh), and me and Grumpy (it's just an act, he's really tender), and me and Sneezy (God bless him), and me and Dopey (I finally found out where his brain is located), and me and . . . and . . . wait a second, there's one more, that's only six. Who is it? Who is it! Dammit.

The Prince

My lawyers have advised me to say nothing, but not-for-publication I can tell you I was appalled. I thought she had just cooked and cleaned for those dwarfs, and the relationship was, shall we say, avuncular. I had no idea. But when Snow White began disappearing every afternoon and I became concerned, her stepmother suggested

66

I engage a private detective. It turned out there were goings-on in that cottage quite unbefitting my wife, the future queen. I have been informed that she was actually having relations with all seven—Doc, Bashful, Grumpy, Sneezy, Happy, Dopey, and, wait, let me think, there's one more. Who's the seventh? Rudolph?

...And Now It's Time to Play Joint Custody

Object: Raising children.

Players: A formerly married couple.

Winner: No one. Game is played for lack of a more satisfying alternative and the pleasure of interacting with one's ex, which no player will admit to.

Game Over: When youngest child turns eighteen.

Scoring: Totals are kept secretly by each player because neither will admit that he or she is playing a game.

Rules: None. Nevertheless each player is convinced that the other is not playing by them.

THE GAME

A player scores by negotiating[1] to his or her advantage
the following issues: Pick Up And Deliver, Holidays,
Sneakers, The Bar Mitzvah Suit, and Extra Weekends
And Vacations.

Pick Up And Deliver. In this category, the object is
to make your ex do the driving. To do this you must
establish that it's more inconvenient for you to pick up
the children than it is for your ex to deliver them. (*See*
Tactics: Playing The Victim.)

Holidays. You are faced with a conflict. Do you want
your children for Thanksgiving or Christmas? You must
secure them for the holiday of your choice. Bonus points
are awarded if you obtain the children for Christmas but
arrange to return them to your ex by December thirty-
first, thereby avoiding the problem of locating a sitter for
New Year's Eve.

Sneakers. You must convince your ex to purchase the
child's new pair of sneakers. Unlike Pick Up And Deliver
or Holidays, the sneaker negotiation is conducted silently.

---

[1]Negotiating: You call your interaction negotiating if you are
winning, which you do not admit to since there are no winners
and, besides, you aren't playing. You call your own interaction
negotiating and you call your opponent's manipulating if you are
losing. You always admit to losing even if you do not admit to
playing. This is because you believe your ex is playing a game in
which you are refusing to participate.

The player wins who is able to ignore the condition of the child's current pair of sneakers longer, thus forcing the ex into laying out the money.

The Bar Mitzvah Suit.[2,3] The object is twofold. You must convince your ex to pay half the cost of the suit, then keep the suit at your house exclusively, making your ex feel that his or her contribution, though equal, was worth less.[4] Danger: A player who refuses to foot half the bill risks retaliation (*see* Revenge). You also risk guilt for refusing to participate in the spiritual life of your child, which is why retaining custody of the bar mitzvah suit is so important: Symbolically, you are retaining custody of Judaism.

Advanced play 1:[5] Get your ex to pay half the cost of the bar mitzvah party.

Advanced play 2: Get your ex to pay the entire cost of the suit. The easiest way to accomplish this is by accident—i.e., if your ex's wedding falls within a month of the bar mitzvah or within a year if the child has not grown. Your ex buys the son a wedding suit, which the son then wears to his bar mitzvah. You win even though no ne-

---

[2]If you are not Jewish, you cannot participate in this negotiation.

[3]If you are Jewish and have a daughter, substitute bat mitzvah dress for bar mitzvah suit.

[4]As opposed to Playing The Victim, which is advantageous in Joint Custody, Being Victimized is not.

[5]Players do not become advanced with practice. Some never get good; others are born that way.

gotiation has taken place because your ex believes you have put one over on him.[6,7]

Extra Weekends And Vacations. The object is to negotiate extra weekends and vacations of your choice with the children. The most successful players are the ones with the best memories and the most relatives.

Example, memory: "Remember when your back was out three years ago and I took the children on your day? Well, next Saturday I need you to take them on mine." (*See also* Tactics, Invoking Past Favors.)

Example, relatives: "I have to have the kids next weekend, their cousins will be in town."

TACTICS

In any negotiation, a player may employ one or more of these tactics: Playing The Victim, Invoking Past Favors, and Intrusion.

[6]Being Victimized is not desirable, but some players desire it anyway.

[7]You should be aware that this is the short version of the game. If you want to play the long version, you can negotiate any issue not covered in the divorce agreement: who pays half the cost of the computer, bicycle, bicycle repair; who goes to Open School Night; who pays for the Brownie uniform, soccer uniform, Little League uniform, wedding, wedding dress, wedding reception; who makes the birthday party this year; who takes the children to the doctor; who buys their school supplies; who accompanies them trick-or-treating.

Playing The Victim.[8] The victim has the edge in any Joint Custody negotiation because of his or her ability to play off the ex's guilt. To play the victim, you must trick your ex into saying these three words: "How are you?"[9] Once these words have been spoken, you are in position to Play The Victim. All you have to do is answer the question.

Sample answer: "While I was taking Katie to the dentist, the brakes on the car went out, on a hill no less, and I had to call Triple A and wait forty minutes for them to come, and then call the dentist and cancel, which I had to do last time because she had the flu, remember (I hope they don't charge me), and then, when I got home, what was in the mail? A letter from the IRS, which took me a good hour even to understand. Something about disallowing a deduction but it's in litigation, does that make sense? Apparently I may owe them more money. Then I picked up Corey, who had a note from his teacher— he spit again. I got home, docked Corey dessert for spitting, and the phone rang. It was my boss. The company might go under this weekend. I'll find out if my job exists on Monday."[10,11]

[8]The most popular tactic.

[9]Who *plays* the victim is not who *is* the victim, but who wants to be. When both players desire the role, the one with the greater gift for it usually secures it.*

*Frequently this is not the victim.

[10]Most advanced players realize that Playing The Victim comes down to one thing: money. It is not enough to imply hardship,

Invoking Past Favors. When negotiating any issue, players should keep in mind that any favor done an ex is a possible trump card. You are urged to remember any time you functioned as a friend—took your ex to the doctor, for example, commiserated over a broken heart, or helped secure a loan. RULE: There are no favors in the game of Joint Custody. There are only chits masquerading as favors.[12]

Intrusion. Intrusion is the art of making your ex feel that he or she is still married to you.[13] This tactic does not affect the negotiation per se. It makes your ex concede without negotiating because he or she is sick of you.

Intrusion takes many forms. One is phoning your ex and asking him to fix the toilet. Another is asking where your ex is going when he or she is leaving town for a few days. A third: When your ex is planning to see a friend that both of you know, you can say, "Give him my love." Other opportunities for Intrusion:

• The flu. When a child has the flu at your ex's house,

---

unless the hardship in some way makes you poorer—not than you were before, but poorer than your ex.

[11]Special effects always help, such as sniffling.

[12]Most players know this instinctively and when doing an ex any favor simultaneously file it away as an IOU to be called in later. Play is at its most natural in Joint Custody when players are Invoking Past Favors.

[13]It should be noted that "intrusion" is a word used only by the player being intruded upon. The intruder calls what he or she is doing other things, like "being friendly."

you can telephone at any time to discuss temperature or medicine, to suggest the child be taken to a doctor, and to find out what the doctor said.[14]

•Drop-Offs. A player has the opportunity to intrude whenever he or she drops a child at the ex's for a visit. You do this by issuing drop-off instructions.[15] Example: When handing over the child and the overnight bag, you may say, "She's tired. Please put her to bed early." Or, "He has a book report to write—be sure he does it."

Importance-of-Mother Counterattack. In bartering vacations, mothers with children under five can make use of this tactic. When the ex-husband suggests the amount of time for which he would like the child, the mother can counter with, "Children under _____ [insert child's age] are too young to leave their mothers for more than _____ [insert preferred time frame]."

TRAPPING

In any negotiation, a player will attempt to back the ex into a corner, causing him or her to say, "I always . . ." or "You never. . . ." This is known as Trapping. Instantly

---

[14]In this case, the intruder calls what he or she is doing "being a conscientious parent."

[15]In this case, the intruder calls what he or she is doing "having open lines of communication."

all negotiation stops and the game moves from Negotiation into Confrontation. At this point, you have two
choices. The first is to go ahead with the confrontation
and put your grudge cards on the table. Note: Though
grudge cards are part of the game, they were collected
before the game began, when the couple was playing
another game, Marriage.

POSSIBLE GRUDGE CARDS

HERS	*HIS*
He got headaches in traffic jams.	She never wanted to drive.
He never showed his feelings.	Whenever I got angry, she cried.
He was always out jogging.	She acted abandoned every time I went jogging.
He always wanted to leave parties early.	Her idea of a good time was to go to a big party and have superficial conversations.
When our baby woke up in the middle of the night, he never wanted to get up.	She refused to understand that I had to go to work in the morning.
He didn't think my work was as important as his work.	She always turned everything into a feminist issue.

He didn't spend enough time with the children.

She didn't understand that I needed my weekends to relax.

He didn't respect me as a person.

She didn't respect my opinion as a parent.

He had an affair.

She drove me to it.

He drove me to it.

She had an affair.

I gave up my career for him.

She stopped working when she had kids and blamed it on me.

He didn't take Lamaze class seriously enough.

She has no sense of humor.

He wasn't romantic enough.

She was always complaining that I wasn't romantic.

He had premature ejaculations.

She was always labeling everything. I just came fast.

He didn't give me orgasms.

She got angry at *me* because *she* didn't have orgasms.

His business associates ignored me when we went out to dinner.

Her business associates ignored me when we went out to dinner.

Whenever we went out with another couple, he never talked. He just waited to be asked questions.

She always got mad just because I'm not comfortable socially.

76

Whenever we went out with another couple, I ended up talking to the boring one.	I had to put up with her best friend's husband.
He never knew who I was—really.	She never knew who I was—really.
He never appreciated me.	She never appreciated me.

Once grudge cards are on the table, players add them up and the one with more grudge cards wins. However, before conceding the negotiation, the player with fewer grudge cards has the option of buying his or her ex's one-upmanship cards and converting them to grudges.

What is a One-upmanship Card? A one-upmanship card is anything that a player has or has done since the divorce that could make the other player jealous. Examples of one-upmanship cards: a trip to Europe, a new house, remodeling the old house, new furniture, remarriage, a new baby.

However, before an opponent can buy a player's one-upmanship cards and convert them to grudges, the player has the option of neutralizing the cards (eliminating the jealousy factor), thereby making them useless as grudges. A neutralizing action is usually in the form of a phrase snuck into an otherwise innocuous conversation.[16]

---

[16]Some players think there are no innocuous conversations in Joint Custody. In that case, any conversation will do.

Examples:

One-upmanship	Neutralizing Comment
A trip to Europe	"It was a business trip."
Remodeling old house	"My parents paid for it."
New furniture	"It was floor samples on sale."
Remarriage	No neutralizing comment is possible. Only option is Playing The Victim. Sound beaten down when announcing, "I got married again."
A new baby	Mention how old you'll be when the child is a teenager. Project the cost of college tuition in the year 2010.[17]

Alternative. If you do not want to put your grudge cards on the table, you can avoid the confrontation altogether and use middlemen for the rest of the game. This ploy is officially known as Speaking Through Children.

---

[17]Players attempting to neutralize one-upmanship cards may find they are playing in vain. An opponent may be so intent on seeing your one-upmanship as his grudge that he will not notice your attempt to neutralize.*

*This probably means your opponent is extremely gifted at Playing The Victim.

Some examples: "Call your mother and ask her when she is coming to pick you up"; "Tell your father I need a check for half your day camp." If your children are under five years of age, this option is not open to you. You must go ahead with the confrontation or take your chances with a telephone tape machine. Avoiding confrontations by leaving messages on your ex's tape machine—"I'm taking the kids to the beach, have them dressed appropriately"—is risky because you can continue the game only when your ex isn't home.

REVENGE

Players are allowed to take revenge but they do not admit it, and it is not called revenge. It is called Being Fair. Example: "If I have to pay the entire cost of college tuition, *it's only fair* that I get to have my address on the child's application."[18] A player of Joint Custody is constantly trying to figure out what revenge to take—what is fair under the circumstances. For instance, let's say your ex will only pay one third of the bar mitzvah party expenses. Should you then restrict your ex to a shorter guest list than you, should you allow your ex to come to the party but not to plan it, should you tell your ex to plan his or her own party, or should you let your ex participate

---

[18]The only problem with revenge in Joint Custody is that your ex may have no idea you are taking it.

in date and time selection but not menu?[19] Sometimes a player opts not to take revenge, preferring instead to complain. This is known as Misplaced Revenge because your friends end up suffering instead of your ex.

Intrusion as Revenge. Intrusion, a tactic, can also be used as revenge, but it is not called Revenge or Being Fair. It is called Putting Your Child's Needs First. Example: Your ex is taking the children on vacation. Call long distance. "Don't let them snorkel without lessons." "Don't let them see *Tarzan, the Legend of Greystoke*—the part with the apes is too scary." In this case, Intrusion has a double impact. Your ex will feel that you are on the vacation too, and—this is the revenge part—even though your ex is the children's parent, he or she isn't competent to take care of them. (For similar results, *see* Tactics, Drop-Offs.)

COMPLICATION CARD: REMARRIAGE

At any time, a player can pick a complication card.[20] Now whenever you negotiate on the phone, your new mate

---

[19]A distinction must be drawn between clean revenge (the above examples) and dirty revenge. Dirty revenge, in the case of the bar mitzvah party, is saying to the child, "Your dad (or mom) is only contributing a third."*
*This revenge is called Revenge, not Being Fair.
[20]A complication card is viewed by your opponent as a one-upmanship card. Sometimes you share this view.

will be in the room with you and, as soon as you finish, tell you what you should have said instead. This may prolong the negotiation—you now have the option of calling back your ex and renegotiating along the lines suggested by your new mate, which may result in Confrontation. If you choose to negotiate when your new mate is not within listening distance, you will still be told how you screwed the whole thing up when you tell your new mate what transpired.

RULE: A remarried player always repeats the details of any joint custody negotiation to his present mate, sometimes several times, and always regrets it.[21]

PENALTY

There is only one penalty in Joint Custody, and it is never recognized as a penalty until after it has taken place. The penalty is called Meeting In A Coffee Shop To Discuss The Children. You will do this in the interests of playing a more effective game but will only succeed in ruining your day. The player who ends up feeling better about the meeting is the one who Played The Victim more successfully. This is also the player who did not pick up the check.

[21]See footnote 6.

81

A Mom's Life

Take your plate into the kitchen, please.
Take it downstairs when you go.
Don't leave it there, take it upstairs.
Is that yours?
Don't hit your brother.
I'm talking to you.
Just a minute, please, can't you see I'm talking?
I said, don't interrupt.
Did you brush your teeth?
What are you doing out of bed?
Go back to bed.
You can't watch in the afternoon.
What do you mean, there's nothing to do?
Go outside.

Read a book.
Turn it down.
Get off the phone.
Tell your friend you'll call her back. Right now!
Hello. No, she's not home.
She's still not home.
She'll call you when she gets home.
Take a jacket. Take a sweater.
Take one anyway.
Someone left his shoes in front of the TV.
Get the toys out of the hall. Get the toys out of the
    bathtub. Get the toys off the stairs.
Do you realize that could kill someone?
Hurry up.
Hurry up. Everyone's waiting.
I'll count to ten and then we're going without you.
Did you go to the bathroom?
If you don't go, you're not going.
I mean it.
Why didn't you go before you left?
Can you hold it?
What's going on back there?
Stop it.
I said, stop it!
I don't want to hear about it.
Stop it, or I'm taking you home right now.
That's it. We're going home.
Give me a kiss.

I need a hug.
Make your bed.
Clean up your room.
Set the table.
I need you to set the table!
Don't tell me it's not your turn.
Please move your chair in to the table.
Sit up.
Just try a little. You don't have to eat the whole thing.
Stop playing and eat.
Would you watch what you're doing?
Move your glass, it's too close to the edge.
Watch it!
More, what?
More, *please*. That's better.
Just eat one bite of salad.
You don't always get what you want. That's life.
Don't argue with me. I'm not discussing this anymore.
Go to your room.
No, ten minutes are not up.
One more minute.
How many times have I told you, don't do that.
Where did the cookies go?
Eat the old fruit before you eat the new fruit.
I'm not giving you mushrooms. I've taken all the mushrooms out. See?
Is your homework done?
Stop yelling. If you want to ask me something, come here.

84

STOP YELLING. IF YOU WANT TO ASK ME SOME-
THING, COME HERE.
I'll think about it.
Not now.
Ask your father.
We'll see.
Don't sit so close to the television, it's bad for your eyes.
Calm down.
Calm down and start over.
Is that the truth?
Fasten your seat belt.
Did everyone fasten their seat belts?
I'm sorry that's the rule. I'm sorry that's the rule. I'm
sorry, that's the rule.

Coping with Santa

Lisa had turned eight in October and as Christmas approached, Santa Claus was more and more on her mind. During the week before Christmas, every night she announced to her father, "I know who really brings the presents. You do!" Then, waiting a moment, she added, "Right?"

Larry didn't answer. Neither he nor I was sure she really wanted the truth. We suspected she did but couldn't bring ourselves to admit it to her. And we both felt uncomfortable saying something hedgy. Something pretentious. Something like, "But Santa does exist, dear. He exists in spirit—in the spirit of giving in all of us." That sounded like some other parents in some other house with some other child.

I actually resented Lisa for putting us on the spot. Wasn't the truth about Santa something one learned from a classmate? The same classmate who knew a screwed-up version of the facts of life. Or else from a know-it-all older sister. Mine sneaked into my room on Christmas Eve, woke me, and said, "Go into the hall and look. You'll see who really puts out the presents."

There was another problem. Larry and I were reluctant to give up Santa Claus ourselves; we didn't want any changes in our Christmas. Every year we go out to a Christmas tree farm in the middle of the San Fernando Valley and, in eighty-degree temperatures, chop down our own tree. This year we misjudged the height and bought an absolutely enormous one. It took four people to get it onto the roof of the car, and then we were so concerned with tying it on securely, with layer upon layer of twine, that we didn't realize, until we finished, that we had tied the car doors closed. All of us—Lisa, Alex, Larry, and I—had to crawl into the car through the windows and out again when we got home. The tree was so heavy that to stand it up, we had to lay it across the living room couch and affix the tree stand while the tree was horizontal; and then, using all our muscle, we had to flip the bottom of the tree down off the couch so that the tree swung into the air. Miraculously it stood, and straight, too.

These adventures were all the more exciting for Larry and me because the kids believed in Santa Claus. We loved to tell them to put out the cookies in case he was hungry. We made a fuss about the fire being out in the fireplace so he wouldn't get burned. We issued a few threats about his list of good children and bad. This was all part of the tension and thrill of Christmas Eve—the night the fantasy comes true. And that fantasy of a fat jolly man who flies through the sky in a sleigh drawn by reindeer and arrives via chimney with the presents—that single belief says everything about the innocence of children. How unbearable to lose it—for them and for us. So Larry and I said nothing to Lisa. And every night, she asked again.

Christmas Eve. Lisa appeared with a sheet of yellow, lined paper. At the top she had written, "If you are real, sign here." It was, she said, a letter to Santa. She insisted that on this letter each of us—her father, Alex, and I— write the words "Santa Claus," so if Santa were to sign it, she could compare our handwriting with his. Then she would know she had not been tricked.

Larry signed. I signed. Alex, who was five and couldn't write, gave up after the letter "S." Lisa folded the paper into quarters, wrote "Santa Claus" on the outside, and stuck it on a ledge inside the chimney along with two Christmas cookies.

After much fuss, Lisa and Alex were tucked into bed. Larry and I put out the presents. We were not sure what to do about the letter.

After a short discussion, and mostly because we couldn't

resist, we opted for deceit. Larry took the note and, in the squiggliest printing imaginable, wrote, "Merry Christmas, Love, Santa Claus." He put the note back in the fireplace and ate the cookies.

The next morning, very early, about six, we heard Lisa and Alex tear down the hall. Larry and I, in bed, listened for the first ecstatic reactions to the presents. Suddenly, we heard a shriek. "He's real! He's real! He's really real!" The door to our room flew open. "He's REAL!" she shouted. Lisa showed us the paper with the squiggly writing.

Somehow, this was not what we had bargained for. I had expected some modicum of disbelief—at least a "Dad, is this for real?"

Lisa clasped the note to her chest. Then she dashed back to the presents.

That afternoon, our friend Alice came over to exchange gifts. "Santa Claus is real," said Lisa.

"Oh," said Alice.

"I know for sure, for really, really sure. Look!" And Lisa produced the proof.

Just then the phone rang. Knowing it was a relative calling with Christmas greetings, Lisa rushed to answer it. "Santa Claus is real," I heard her say to my sister, the same sister who had broken the bad news about Santa Claus to me thirty years ago. Lisa handed me the phone.

"What is this about?" asked my sister.

I told her the story, trying to make it as funny as possible, hoping she wouldn't notice how badly Larry and

I had handled what I was beginning to think of as "the Santa issue." It didn't work.

"We may have made a mistake here," said my sister, diplomatically including herself in the mess.

"You're telling me!" I said. "Do you think there's any chance Lisa will forget all this?" That's what I really wanted—for the whole thing to go away.

"I doubt it," said my sister.

Bedtime. "Dad?" said Lisa, as he tucked her in.

"What?"

"If Santa's real, then Rudolph must be real too."

"What?"

"If Santa's real—"

"I heard," said Larry. He sat down on her bed and took a deep breath. "You know, Lisa—" and then he stopped. I could see he was trying to think of a way, any way, to explain our behavior so it wouldn't sound quite as stupid as it was. But he was stumped.

"Yeah," said Lisa.

"I wrote the note," said Larry.

She burst into tears.

Larry apologized. He apologized over and over while Lisa sobbed into her pillow. He said he was wrong, that he shouldn't have tricked her, that he should have answered her questions about Santa Claus the week before.

Lisa sat up in bed. "I thought he was real," she said reproachfully. Then suddenly she leaned over the bed, pulled out a comic from underneath, and sat up again. "Can I read for five minutes?" she said.

"Sure," said Larry.

And that was it. One minute of grief at Santa's death, and life went on.

Larry and I left Lisa's room terribly relieved. I immediately got a craving for leftover turkey and headed for the kitchen. I was putting the bird back in the refrigerator when I heard Alex crying. I went down the hall. The door to his room was open and I heard Lisa, very disgusted, say, "Oh, Alex, you don't have to cry. Only babies believe in Santa Claus."

Mr. Flanta

We arrived home from a vacation to discover that all the electricity in the house was out. I will not go into how, when you come home from a vacation, it's always something. We called Mr. Flanta.

The last time Mr. Flanta had been at our house, we had needed a light installed on the patio. By the time he was finished, we had agreed to three lights on the patio, a light in the garage, a new front door light, and a light in the hall closet. Mr. Flanta had demonstrated how the closet light worked: He turned on the patio switch, walked inside the house, opened the closet door, and flipped on the switch in the closet.

"Wait a minute," I had said. "Do you mean that in

order to turn on the light in the closet, I first have to turn on the patio light?"

"Is necessary," said Mr. Flanta, whose English is not all that it might be.

Why, you may wonder, were we calling him again? It was a Saturday night and he was the only electrician we knew. Also he is cheap, which is fortunate: By the time we agree to the extras he inevitably suggests, we have exceeded our budget anyway.

Which brings me to a problem I have. Whenever I hire an electrician (or anyone else in the home repair or improvement category), things get out of hand. Either, like Mr. Flanta, the person points out things he can do for me for just a little more money, things that are in addition to what I want and that I suddenly can't imagine I ever lived without; or he explains that what I think of as a simple job is not simple at all. The tree man comes to pull out the hydrangea bush and delivers a twenty-minute lecture on the tenaciousness of hydrangea roots—how they're probably tangled in the camellia or the house pipes or goodness knows what else that even I with my tendency to project disaster had never thought of. All this by way of preparation for the cost estimate. But the estimate, high as it might be, is always a lot less anxiety-producing than the buildup. Maybe that's the point.

In the clutches of these experts, Larry and I have trouble saying no. Well, to be honest, Larry is a lot worse than I am. Once a man appeared at our door and told Larry that for thirteen dollars he would paint our address on our driveway. Not on the curb where everyone else on the block has his address, but directly on the driveway. He pointed out the advantage: Our house could be spotted from a helicopter. Presumably, the police would have an easier time either rescuing us or arresting us. Larry immediately handed over the money, and when I arrived home, the man had just finished painting black numbers, about a foot high, on a white rectangle. Our house looked as if it were about to have its mug shot taken. I was only able to scrub the numbers off before they dried because a carpenter, who was at our house explaining why he was six months late building our bookshelves, happened to have some very strong paint remover in his truck.

I suppose Larry and I are an easy touch. There is probably a home improvement newsletter, to the trade only, that advises all out-of-work repair people to head for our house. But I suspect our problem is more serious than that. This confusion—who's in charge here, me or the tree man?—indicates some lack of maturity. It does not, for instance, seem like a situation my parents would have found themselves in.

Not that my parents were perfect examples of grown-ups, but they did manage to accomplish a few things I can't, like calling their doctors by their first names. I only attempted this in the past year and still not with my gynecologist. My father, especially, always took a possessive, paternalistic attitude toward anyone he was paying for service. It may have been condescending, but when people did work for my father, they instantly became "his." For example, after having his living room lamps rewired, my father referred to the man in the shop as "my lamp man." I always have the feeling that people who do work for me are not mine, but that I am somehow theirs. I fear at least some of them share this opinion. How else to explain the painters, *my* painters (three women—one ex-nun, one ex-lawyer, one ex-reporter), asking me to throw a cocktail party for them so they could raise money to buy land in Michigan and study the roots of lesbianism?

Which is all by way of saying that I was not looking forward to the arrival of Mr. Flanta. We prepared for the worst. Preparing for the worst is an activity I have taken up since I turned thirty-five and the worst actually began to happen. "Perhaps the whole house needs rewiring," I said. "Well, big deal, we go into hock." Pointing out that the worst is bearable (when it is) is also something I have taken up post thirty-five. My husband and I agreed in advance, knowing that an answer might be required on the spot, that if Mr. Flanta did say the house needed rewiring, we would get a second opinion. We formulated this plan in the pathetic hope of maintaining control, but it quickly became clear that we had underestimated the power of the opposition.

Mr. Flanta is about sixty, tiny and unfailingly polite.

Between the light-in-the-closet incident and the present lights-on-the-blink incident, he had had open-heart surgery. I realized this the second he walked in because his shirt was open three buttons and I could see the scar. Also he mentioned it. Feeling concern for his well-being instantly put me at a disadvantage. So did his limited English. It stands to reason that if I have trouble asserting myself, I will have even more trouble if the person I am speaking to doesn't understand what I say.

The first thing Mr. Flanta did was proceed to the fuse box, where he found a screw loose. He tightened it and all the lights in the house went on. This was too good to be true, it turned out, for a few minutes later we discovered that one room, an upstairs bedroom, was still blacked out. Mr. Flanta concluded that there must be a short circuit and we would have to try all the plugs and appliances to find out where (or which). "Mr. Hart," he said to my husband, "you go in kitchen. I go in yard. You wait. When I say, 'Hold it,' then you do it."

Do it? Do what? I had no idea what he was talking about, but Larry acted as if he did. He went right into the kitchen; I followed. Mr. Flanta yelled, "Hold it." Larry unplugged the toaster.

"I think he wants you to turn it on," I said.

"But he said 'Hold it,' " said Larry.

I went back into the yard. "Mr. Flanta," I said, "I don't understand."

"Is very simple," said Mr. Flanta. "You go in kitchen.

I stay in yard. You wait. When I say, 'Hold it,' then you do it."

"Do you want me to turn on all the appliances?"

"Yes," said Mr. Flanta.

"Okay." I went back inside.

"Hold it," he yelled. We turned on the dishwasher. Since we had received no instructions about what to do next, and since Larry and I had the same inclination—given whom we were dealing with, we would rather guess than ask—we waited a second, then turned the dishwasher off.

And on we went—Mr. Flanta yelling "Hold it," and Larry and I turning on one appliance and light switch after another. At one point Mr. Flanta made an appearance. "Remember the order," he said. This was not remotely a possibility, but fortunately it never came up again. Finally I got to the vacuum cleaner and saw a burnt spot around the plug. "Aha!" said Mr. Flanta, when we showed it to him. "This is it. Or maybe not." He plugged in the vacuum. It worked perfectly. Mr. Flanta then decided there must be an unknown fuse box, a sort of mystery fuse box, in the house, and he spent several minutes checking closets, basement, even cupboards. Nothing. He went upstairs to the blacked-out room. He noticed a fuse lying on the table, picked it up, and examined it. "No good, throw away," he said, handing it to Larry.

"But Mr. Flanta, this is new. I just took it out of the package."

Mr. Flanta examined it again. "Is good, put away." He gave it back to Larry.

Then he looked out the window. "Aha!" (Now that I had spent some time with Mr. Flanta, I knew what this meant: "This is it. Or maybe not.") He had spotted three wires running from the garage to just under the window outside this room.

"Please, Mr. Hart, I show you." Larry followed him downstairs and outside. He stationed Larry at the garage on a stepladder. "We have three wires—one, two, three. I go upstairs and pull. You tell me which one."

He went upstairs. Larry watched the wires. Mr. Flanta came down again. "Which one?" he asked.

"None of them," said Larry. Mr. Flanta went back again.

Now Mr. Flanta was running up and down the stairs, pulling wires that Larry was unable to identify. I began to be terrified that Mr. Flanta would have a heart attack. On the fourth trip, Mr. Flanta said, "Is a nightmare, but maybe we have a miracle." The only miracle I could imagine was the sudden disappearance of Mr. Flanta. It was clear to me that Larry and I had done an inadequate job of preparing for the worst. We had no plan to accommodate a mad electrician with a heart condition.

Finally Mr. Flanta gave up on the wires and took apart all the outlets in the blacked-out room. When that didn't pan out either, he decided the problem had to be in the ceiling. He would return Wednesday, and, for $250, rewire the entire room. It was the longest buildup to an

98

estimate I had ever heard. Then Mr. Flanta discovered his pliers were lost, had some apple juice, and left.

Larry and I collapsed at the breakfast table. Larry started laughing. I couldn't believe he was laughing. I felt as if a tornado had just been in the house and we should be on our knees to God, thanking him for our having survived it.

"I have an idea," I said. "Why don't you call up Mr. Flanta tonight, ask him how much we owe him, and tell him that we won't be needing him again?" I said this really casually, thinking perhaps Larry wouldn't notice what a terrible job I had just given him.

"Are you kidding?" said Larry. "I'm not doing that. Why don't you?"

I considered it. I considered Mr. Flanta: his surgery; his height—under 5 feet 4 inches; the fact that, given this limited demonstration, he probably knows very little about electricity. Yes, there was no doubt about it: He was not *my* electrician; I was *his* customer.

"I think we should prepare for the worst," I said to Larry. "Let's increase our fire insurance."

At the Club

11:00 A.M. We put our towels in the trunk. I announce that everyone has to bring something to read because we are going to be at the club all day. All of them—Lisa, Alex, their cousin Andrew, thirteen years old, and Lisa's friend Kim—go back into the house complaining.

11:20 A.M. We pull into the club parking lot. Kim shrieks and ducks her head behind the seat. "That's Jason's car," she says.

"Who's Jason?"

"He was my boyfriend in the second grade."

"He drives already?"

"No. He's twelve."

I say that it probably isn't Jason's parents' car—lots of people have green Volvos.

11:45 A.M. The kids go swimming. I sit down to relax and realize that I forgot to bring something to read. I take Andrew's book, *I Tell a Lie Every So Often,* by Bruce Clements. On the cover it says that the hero is a fourteen-year-old boy and the year is 1848.

NOON. Jason is spotted. Kim says she won't speak to him unless he speaks to her first.

12:05 P.M. Alex takes his helicopter into the pool and is thrown out because toys are not allowed. In the book I am reading, the hero's brother learns that his girlfriend, Caroline, pads her undergarments to make her bosom look bigger.

12:45 P.M. The kids are hungry. I decide that I would rather not eat lunch than eat with them. I send them up to the club coffee shop. In the book, the hero tells his brother that a white girl with red hair is living with an Indian tribe in Dakota territory. The brother thinks it must be their cousin who disappeared one night when she went outside to go to the bathroom.

12:50 P.M. The kids come back from the coffee shop

outraged. "We have to wear shoes," says Lisa. "It's so unfair," says Kim. They put them on and go back.

1:00 P.M. The hero and his brother leave on a boat to find their missing cousin. I put a towel on my lounge chair because my legs are getting crisscross marks on them.

1:30 P.M. I go into the coffee shop to check on the kids. They are speculating on the identity of a piece of white asparagus in Lisa's chef salad. Kim is sure it's a leek. Every time she says the word, they have hysterics laughing.

Andrew says, "Should we tip a lot 'cause—"

Lisa butts in. "We were playing, well, not really, only sort of, and my Coke fell over—"

Andrew: "The waiter was really nice and brought another so we thought—"

"Throw in at least another quarter," says Lisa to Andrew decisively.

"Tip twenty percent," I say. "That'll be four dollars." I leave them eating ice cream and go back to my book. The boat the hero and his brother are traveling on sinks but everyone is saved. I get splashed by some teenagers doing cannonballs off the board and change seats.

2:00 P.M. The kids come back from the coffee shop— Lisa furious in front; Alex, looking sheepish, trailing behind.

Lisa: "Alex said a prejudiced remark to the waiter."

"Alex, is this true?"

Alex just stands there.

"Alex, sit down. You're not going swimming for a while."

Lisa says, "Well, it wasn't really prejudiced. It was only sort of prejudiced."

"Was it or wasn't it?"

"Only sort of," says Lisa. "I think maybe only for ten minutes he shouldn't be allowed to swim."

"I'll decide that. Alex, stay here. Everyone else go into the pool."

Alex sits down. "All I said was I didn't want that guy to be our waiter because he wasn't nice and made us wear shoes."

Obviously I am not getting the whole story. "Did you say anything about his being Mexican?"

"No."

I deliver a lecture just in case. "Alex, this is very important. It's perfectly okay to say that someone isn't nice if you think they're rude, but you never, ever criticize anyone for where they came from, their religion, or the color of their skin."

And Alex says, in a singsong voice indicating he's repeating something he's heard only about seven thousand times, "It's not how people look that matters, it's what they're like inside." I tell him to go swimming.

2:45 P.M. The hero's brother announces that he's going to marry Caroline's sister. I don't remember ever reading

103

that he and Caroline broke up and spend the next twenty minutes trying to find the place in the book where that happened. Alex is thrown out of the pool again for trying to take his helicopter in.

3:10 P.M. Lisa convinces me that she's allowed in the Jacuzzi, even though a sign says, "No one allowed in Jacuzzi under sixteen years of age." She does this by pointing out another sign, "Women in pool must wear bathing caps at all times," and the fact that the women in the pool are capless.

3:15 P.M. Lisa is thrown out of the Jacuzzi.

3:30 P.M. The hero and his brother are told they can identify their missing cousin by a wen on her back. I stop reading to eavesdrop on a conversation of three women discussing television habits. One would never have the set on if her husband didn't watch. Another says her husband falls asleep ten minutes after turning on the set, every time. The third says a friend in her office tapes the soaps every day and watches them at night.

3:40 P.M. Lisa takes Alex's plastic action figure and pretends to pull its head off. Alex yells, "Delia, Lisa's killing Manton Two." I ignore him and go back to reading.

4:00 P.M. The hero and his brother head for a place called

Vermillion where a redheaded white girl reportedly is living with her Indian uncle. A preacher says that she could not be their cousin because she does not look like a turtle and everyone in their cousin's family looks like a turtle.

4:15 P.M. Lisa asks for a candy bar from the machine. I ask her to find out how much they cost.

4:18 P.M. Lisa comes running. "Good news. At some places they cost fifty cents but here they cost only forty." I give her enough money for everyone and tell her not to run near the pool.

4:20 P.M. Alex comes running to say that Lisa told him to tell me that the machine is out of Snickers bars. I tell him not to run near the pool.

4:30 P.M. The hero and his brother track the girl to a lake where she is swimming, but they do not succeed in spotting the wen. Instead of shooting an Indian as planned, the brother shoots the hero. It is only a flesh wound, but it puts an end to their adventure. All the kids return eating Munch bars.

4:45 P.M. I announce we're leaving.
    Lisa: "Can we go to the movies now?"

"I think you've had enough for one day."

"Please."

"There isn't time. Your dad and I are going to the movies ourselves tonight."

On the way to the car, Lisa says to Kim, "It's not fair. Parents have all the fun."

Hair

When a friend of mine got divorced, he got custody of his son's hair. This was not spelled out in the separation agreement. In fact, my friend had no idea that his son's hair was in his custody until one day, during his three and a half days with his children, he took his daughter for a haircut and shortly thereafter returned both children for their three and a half days with their mother. Their mother, his ex-wife, went berserk. She said he was not allowed to take their daughter for a haircut. Ever. He could take the son; she would take the daughter.

At the time, I assumed this story was just another example of the way divorced couples turn everything into a battleground, even the hair on their children's heads. Or else it was about the way divorced couples pretend

to be fair—you take the son, I'll take the daughter—
when they are really being competitive, like siblings. It
sometimes seems as if divorce changes husband and wife
into brother and sister. Their child, or children, is the
single bottle of Coca-Cola they are splitting equally, each
panicked the other will get more. One couple I know
even divided up their daughter's wedding march. One
took her halfway down the aisle and the other, the rest
of the way.

I interviewed about twenty-five children of divorced
parents while writing this book and I often heard them
say, "I was split apart" or "ripped apart" in describing the
effect of the divorce. At first I assumed they meant that
they had been emotionally shattered, but as I heard those
words again and again I came to think they were describing some inner divorce of their own selves. Every child
who still saw both parents regularly told me he behaved
differently at each house. The rules, spoken and unspo-
ken, were different; the food was different—some ate
wheat germ and Tiger's Milk at one home and Cheetos
at the other. They asked for things differently. To get
something as small as an ice cream cone or as important
as approval they had to present themselves in different
ways. This is a sophisticated talent, very useful in some
professional work, but not something I associate with
childhood or with innocence. In a sense, having been
split apart, the child of divorce became two people.

Or else, I suppose, he could be thought of as a middle child between a brother and sister, his parents. He is trying to make the adjustments necessary to get along with each.

In any event, since I assumed my friend's haircut story to be some form of insane sibling rivalry between exes, I didn't pay too much attention to it. I was more taken with his story about how his ex-wife sent him the bill for having the cat fixed because she claimed it came under the category of medical expenses, which, according to the separation agreement, he was responsible for. But later, during interviews with divorced parents, hair kept turning up as a source of conflict. I should not have been surprised. I came of age in the sixties when young men grew long hair as a way to proclaim their politics and insult their parents: "I am not what you are." Hair symbolized the generation gap. Now I was finding it symbolized the divorce gap.

In my interviews, the first "hair issue" between exes I noticed might be called the Same Sex Hair Problem, of which my friend's ex-wife was a prime example. Like her, several mothers insisted on being responsible for their daughter's hair, and several fathers, for their son's. Or put another way, several mothers did not want their ex-husbands messing with their daughter's hair; several fathers did not want their ex-wives messing with their son's. I did not, in my unscientific survey, encounter a situation in which a parent of one sex insisted on controlling the hair of an opposite-sex child.

Curious to know what this meant, I called a psychologist living in Berkeley, California, where hair first started growing in the sixties. She speculated that the Same Sex Hair Problem has to do with the inability of some parents to see their children as separate from themselves—they can't distinguish where their child's hair ends and theirs begins. This over-identification would more logically occur when parent and child are the same sex. So when my friend got his daughter a haircut, possibly his ex-wife felt he was giving *her* a haircut, in which case the fact that the hair was a little too short and not exactly what she had in mind was more of an affront than was immediately apparent. No woman wants a bad haircut from her ex-husband. It's one more way to feel mistreated. It could even be construed as an attack on her femininity. Likewise, if a man confuses himself with his son, maybe he feels like Samson: His ex-wife is emasculating him when she gets their son a trim.

The second hair issue I noticed—which I call the Hair Priority Syndrome—involved a group of men paying child support. These men were concerned about keeping their children's hair neat and trimmed, but said their ex-wives weren't. While I have expressed this simply, however, the men did not. "Hair is not my ex-wife's priority," said one. "We are people who care about hair," said another of himself and his new wife (meaning his ex-wife wasn't). In this syndrome, an attitude toward a trim is used exactly as it was in the sixties, as a symbol of different values. And—by implication in this case—of how unsuited the couple was to have been married in the first place and how right to be divorced.

The solution to the problem would seem obvious. The man cares about hair so he takes the child for a cut. If you think that, you have never been divorced. For one thing, it's too simple, logical, and straightforward. For another, these former husbands and wives are not simply fighting about hair. It just appears that way because that's all they're talking about. They're also fighting about money.

These men were paying child support. So when one said, "Hair is not my ex-wife's priority," he was actually saying, "My ex-wife won't spend *my* money, which I intended to be for haircuts, on haircuts." (Child support, though paid to the wife, is not considered to be her money, at least not by her ex. She is just the vein through which it flows.) Naturally, the ex-husband cannot just take the child for a haircut because then he would be paying twice— once for the child's haircut, once for the ex-wife to take the child for a haircut. His ex-wife would be making money off him, which she already is since she got money for a haircut that she didn't spend on a haircut. What is she doing with all the child support money anyway? God knows, he can't see it on his children's backs.

So what does the ex-husband do? Does he discuss the hair problem in person, send a note, or say to the child, "Tell Mommy you need a haircut"? It doesn't matter. His ex-wife has no intention of taking the child to the barber. She has not let their child's hair get too long by oversight; his fingernails may be too long by oversight, but not his hair. For like me, most of these women came of age in the sixties and know the symbolic importance of hair. So do their ex-husbands. This is why these men are so distressed about an inch or two of extra hair—a trifle compared to the half-foot of extra hair their own parents may have had to contend with on them. But these couple of inches mean nothing less than who has custody. If a child's hair is styled "your way"—reflecting your values—you know to whom the child really belongs regardless of what it says in the divorce agreement. The haircut is like a brand: This child is mine. And—much more important: This child is not yours. Look how far we've come. In the sixties, men used hair to insult their parents; now their ex-wives use it to insult them.

To put the kindest interpretation on all this childishness, both parents, in overreacting to hair, are probably reacting to loss. The father who doesn't live with his child anymore sees an unacceptable hairdo as yet another reminder of how little influence he now has. A mother who drops her child off at her ex's—to another life—may subconsciously feel in danger of losing the child altogether. So she puts a brand on the child's head to indicate where the child came from and where the child belongs.

There are not many features on a child's body a parent can style in his own image, but shortly after my friend upset his ex-wife by getting their daughter a haircut, his ex-wife had their daughter's ears pierced. My friend suspected—no, he was sure—it was retaliation.

Visitation

Have dinner with Dad and special friend he wants you to meet. When he asks afterward if you liked her, say, "She was okay." Take all clothes that are supposed to be left at Dad's back to Mom's.

Go to school play. Sit with Mom for half; switch seats and sit with Dad.

Your stepfather wants Chinese food for dinner. Explain that you don't know why, you just don't feel like eating that kind of food. Your mom will say, "Oh, come on. You like egg rolls." Absolutely refuse. Pick a food your stepfather doesn't want to eat, like hamburgers, and insist that you won't eat anything else.

Get Dad in to see your room at Mom's, go to movies with Dad, have dinner, and refuse to discuss feelings. Ask for a dog. Your dad will say he doesn't want one but why don't you have one at your mom's. Return to Mom's. Ask her if she will get you a dog. She will say, no, but if your dad wants to have one, fine.

Get Mom in to see your room at Dad's.

Beg your mom to let you stay up an hour later just this once. Just when she is about to give in, your stepfather says, "She said 'No' and that's the end of it." Yell "Mind your own business," run to your room, and slam the door. Have fantasy: Stepfather falls off cliff. Mom and Dad get back together.

Tell Mom report card was sent to Dad. Tell Dad report card was sent to Mom.

Your stepfather's two children come to visit. Decide that your mom gives more food at dinner to them than to you. No one watches their butter intake. They get to lie around watching football on TV all day, but you're not allowed to watch one cartoon show in the afternoon. When they do chores, your mom says you have to help them. Yell, "It's not fair. They mess up my room and I have to clean it."

Get stepfather in to see your room at Dad's.

Go to movie with Dad and his girlfriend. Convince him to let you ride in the front seat of the car and make her ride in the back. Complain that you don't want to look in a store when she does, and sulk when she just takes a second to try on a blouse. If the saleslady says, "That looks nice on your mom," say, "That's not my mom." When your dad insists that you give his girlfriend a kiss good night, do it but think it's disgusting, you don't even know her. Wash mouth immediately after. Check in morning to see if she's still around.

Get hamsters at Dad's on condition from Mom that they stay there and never come to her house.

Get Dad's girlfriend in to see your room at Mom's.

Perform in School Sing. Notice that your mom and dad are sitting together. Have fantasy: While Mom and Dad are at School Sing, your stepfather and Dad's girlfriend meet and fall in love. Your mom and dad are heartbroken. They comfort each other. One thing leads to another. They get back together.

Get mad at Mom. Call Dad, crying hysterically, and say you want to live with him.

Your stepbrothers are visiting again. Think that even though your mom and stepfather call them your stepbrothers, it's just a word, and they're really not in your family no matter what anyone says. Think that if you hum for a second after saying the word "stepbrother," that means you didn't even say the word to begin with. Besides, they never play with you. Listen to your stepfather tell them to include you. Refuse to be included. When one of your stepbrothers says, "What's wrong now? We're being nice and you're not being nice back," tell him that they were only being nice because they were forced to. It isn't as though they're being nice for real.

Go to Dad's for weekend but leave favorite shirt at Mom's. Beg Dad to take you back to Mom's to get it. Mope. Whine. Say you've been planning all week to wear it today. Nothing else fits. Everything else is too small for you. Get him to take you.

Move hamsters to Mom's because your dad's girlfriend is allergic to fur. Have fantasy: Dad's girlfriend dies of fur poisoning. Stepfather attends funeral, falls into grave, and is buried alive. Your mom and dad get back together.

Have an argument with Mom about whether you can skip ballet class this week. Worry that your stepfather will interfere again. The entire time you are trying to convince her that you're too tired, hope that he please, please, please keeps his big mouth shut.

Have argument with Dad. His girlfriend takes your side. Wonder if she's trying to play up to you. Have fantasy: Dad gets furious with girlfriend for taking your side. They break up. At that exact moment, stepfather dies in a car crash. Your mom and dad get back together.

Celebrate your birthday with your mom and stepfather. Blow out the candles and wish that your mom and dad would get back together.

Celebrate your birthday with your dad and his girlfriend. Blow out the candles and wish that your mom and dad would get back together. Stare at your dad's girlfriend when you think she isn't looking. Wonder why her hair's so ugly. Wonder why she never shaves under her arms.

She is not as cute as your mom, that's for sure. Eat the chocolate cake that she made. Think, Well, at least she makes good cake.

Go to the school Science Fair. Your mom is there with your stepfather. Your dad is there with his girlfriend. Notice how different your mom and dad are. They don't like to do the same things. They don't like the same music. They don't like the same movies. They don't even eat the same things. Wonder how they were ever married. Think, I used to wish they would get back together, but now I know that's impossible. Have fantasy: Your mom changes to be like your dad (or your dad changes to be like your mom). They get back together.

Ex-Husbands
for Sale

Are you worried about running out of things to talk about?
Are you worried that one day you will sit down to dinner
with your husband or boyfriend and not have a single
thing to say? BUY AN EX-HUSBAND AND KISS THIS
WORRY GOODBYE—for you will find that you are
always talking about him. You will even say the same
things about him over and over and never bore yourself,
continuing to find your comments fascinating and insight-
ful. Some possible topics: How much you hate him. How
happy you would be if he disappeared off the face of the
earth. How thrilled you would be if he got a job in Ku-
wait. Why all the children's sneakers disappear at his house.
Whether he will pay half the cost of your daughter's Sweet
Sixteen party and what it will say about him if he won't.

Is your son developing bad habits? Too much television? Too much sugar? Blame it on the ex—he spoils him on weekends. Do any of your son's personality traits displease you? Is he reluctant to discuss his emotions? Is he unwilling to share? Is he fussy? Will he only wear socks that have no seam at the toe? "That's not my genes," you can say, or "He didn't get that from me." With an ex-husband in the picture, the chip will never be off YOUR block unless YOU want it. AND FURTHERMORE . . .

You need never again feel responsible for your child's misbehavior at school. When the teacher calls to complain, you will suspect that the child is only acting up because he has problems with his father, your handy ex. You can even say, "He's always difficult right after he comes back from his dad's." Or, alternatively, "He's always difficult when he hasn't seen his father enough." If the teacher insists on a parent conference, we guarantee that your ex-husband will either refuse to attend, confirming your worst opinion of him, or attend, ensuring that you will never get anxious about your child's problems EVEN WHILE THE TEACHER IS ENUMERATING THEM. Instead you will be distracted by your ex, thinking, Why does he bitch all the time about paying child support when he can afford a Burberry raincoat?

And to show you just how terrific this offer is, WE ALSO PROMISE . . .

•Lifetime interference in your love life. Anytime you have planned a romantic weekend alone with the new man in your life, your ex-husband will cancel his plans to take the children. He can also, in our more deluxe model, arrive late to pick them up EVERY SINGLE WEEKEND THAT HE DOES TAKE THEM, ensuring that even though you get to be alone with your sweetheart, your plans for the day will be ruined. ALSO . . .

• Lifetime rage at a man you are not married to. This value is not to be underestimated, for it means that any new husband you acquire need never be the focus of your generalized man-hating tendencies, which you wouldn't have anyway if you hadn't married your ex. Yes, we promise that if you supply the anger and resentment, your ex-husband will channel it. ALSO . . .

• Belief in your own sainthood. For putting up with him.

• If possible, a higher self-image. Believing your ex-husband to be irresponsible, irrational, and childish will undoubtedly lead you to conclude that you are responsible, rational, and mature. This is known as the EX-HUSBAND EFFECT.

• Someone to measure your life by. Who has more money? Better values? A better job? A bigger house? Whose new mate is more attractive? Who remarried first? Who was smart enough to wait a while? Whose life is more stable? Whose life is more boring? If you can come out ahead in comparison to your ex-husband, you win the honor of being THE ONE WHO BENEFITED MORE FROM THE DIVORCE.

• A perpetual source of private amusement. His tie is

crooked; he's suddenly becoming religious; he went on a raft river trip; he's gaining weight. To you these things are hysterically funny. In fact, the more ridiculous you can find your ex-husband the better, for it is proof of your great intelligence—you were right to have divorced him.

But wait, THERE'S MORE . . .

A ONE-MONTH, UNCONDITIONAL, MONEY-BACK TRIAL SEPARATION during which your new ex-husband will telephone you every single morning before eight and every evening after ten. You will never know what he is going to say and it will always upset you. Such as (1) he's calling his lawyer tomorrow to put a clause in the settlement that you can never go out of town with the children without his permission; (2) he's finally figured out what went wrong with your marriage; (3) why didn't you consult him on the selection of baby gym class when you supposedly have joint custody?

AND, TO MAKE ABSOLUTELY SURE YOU GET ALL THE RESULTS POSSIBLE FROM YOUR EX, we will include free A BONUS INSTRUCTION BOOK-LET, which tells you, among other things, how to use your ex-husband to control the behavior of your new husband.

Let's say one day your new husband walks into the kitchen and sees the milk sitting on the counter, and no one around planning to drink it. He will say, "Is this milk out for a reason?" He will say this even though he knows the answer. It is his own private joke—the milk is out because you forgot to put it back. Ha, ha. Do not waste any time. Lose your temper immediately and generalize. Inform him that your ex-husband was always saying things like that and give examples, like, "Is the oven on for a reason?" or "Is the flame on under the coffeepot for a reason?" If possible, cry, saying that your ex-husband was always putting you down. Any overreaction will be understandable if an ex-husband is involved, and you can be sure from now on your new husband will put the milk back himself and keep quiet about it. No husband ever wants to resemble an ex-husband. This is one of the best reasons to have an ex-husband around.

And if we still haven't convinced you that what you need is an ex-husband, we would like to point out this unique advantage: YOU WILL NEVER HAVE TO FEEL YOUR EX-HUSBAND IS A REAL PERSON WITH REAL FEELINGS. This is known as THE DIVORCE EFFECT. He is simply the sum of his less attractive parts, a sort of cartoon character: THE EX. So you don't have to feel sympathy for him. He's having trouble with his business? He's short of money? You won't believe it for a minute. You know he's only saying this to get out of paying money to you. And this brings us to the best part: Even though an ex-husband is not real, YOU GET TO TAKE EVERYTHING HE SAYS OR DOES PERSON-ALLY. He brings your child home late? He's doing it to bug you. He goes to Paris? It's just to show off because you always wanted to go to Paris when you were married to him. He breaks his leg so he can't take the kids while you vacation? It's a plot to prevent you from going. Then he has to spend months immobilized in a toe-to-hip cast? How ridiculous. He's just trying to make your friends, who blamed him for the divorce, feel sympathy for him now.

SO CALL OUR TOLL-FREE NUMBER RIGHT NOW and take advantage of this great opportunity to get an ex of your own. Don't settle for listening to your best friend discuss hers. We offer one easy payment plan: Buy now and pay for the rest of your life.

B-E-V-E-R-L-Y

High school is a place I left with more relief than I left anything else in life, except possibly my first marriage. Actually, it occurs to me now that graduating from high school was my sole preparation for divorce. A rehearsal in walking away and never looking back. Of course when I left my marriage, I left a man. When I left high school, I left myself—the self-conscious adolescent who inhabited those four years. I never wanted to feel like that person again. To make sure, I threw the friendships out with the memories, knowing that the former would result in an unfortunate encounter with the latter. I spent twenty years crossing streets to avoid people I went to high school with. I once left an entire week's groceries in the supermarket when I realized that I was standing in the checkout

line behind our class's basketball princess. I once spent
an entire meal in a French restaurant with my hand artfully
placed to conceal my face when I realized that my former
date to the Pigskin Prom was dining at the next table. So
when an invitation to my twentieth high school reunion
arrived in the mail, I was shocked to find myself excited,
even dying to go and see—but what I couldn't imagine.

My school was Beverly Hills High, but in Beverly Hills
terms our class has been a disappointment. Celebrity
graduates from other years include Richard Dreyfuss,
Richard Chamberlain, Bonnie Franklin, Carrie Fisher, Rob
Reiner, Marlo Thomas, Albert Brooks, and André Previn.
We, the class of '62, produced not one star, only a starlet
who appeared in several Kung Fu epics. She achieved
most of her renown by dating Henry Kissinger. Of course,
like most Beverly High classes, ours had its quota of
"children of stars." There was Peter Ford, son of Glenn;
Claudia Martin, daughter of Dean; and Amanda Levant,
daughter of Oscar. But there was no one to compare in
either fame or notoriety to Cheryl Crane, Lana Turner's
daughter, who was in the class ahead of us.

Shortly before entering Beverly, Cheryl Crane stabbed
and killed Johnny Stompanato, a reputed gangster and
her mother's lover. I remember this because, aside from
the scandal, Cheryl sat next to me during I.Q. testing.
She had just been acquitted of the crime on the grounds
of justifiable homicide—she believed she was protecting
her mother—and her presence interfered with my con-

centration. Also, I recall, a popular teenage activity was
to drive by Lana Turner's house and guess which window
was part of the all-pink bedroom the stabbing had taken
place in. So in one sense, at least, Beverly Hills teenagers
were like any others. Typically teenage in that we displayed remarkably little empathy toward Cheryl. Nothing
seemed very sad, tragic, or even real unless it happened
to each of us, directly.

But though we may have displayed characteristic adolescent self-absorption, Beverly Hills kids were different. At least we believed we were special. And this was
in large measure a result of growing up in Beverly Hills.

Beverly Hills, while in the middle of Los Angeles geo-
graphically, is a separate city. It has its own school system,
fire department, and police department. It is often said
that Beverly Hills police are so vigilant that one is stopped
and questioned simply for taking a walk; in spite of having
spacious, perfectly paved sidewalks, people in Beverly
Hills rarely use them, and walking on residential streets
is considered suspicious behavior. I was never stopped
when walking, but I was questioned several times when
necking, parked on the street at night in front of my
house. This was excruciatingly embarrassing, but it nevertheless reinforced the notion that Beverly Hills kids were
well taken care of, better taken care of than anyone else,
which in our adolescent world meant the rest of Los Angeles.

So we were protected, isolated (but in the center of

town, which made it more noticeable), and wealthy—for the most part children of well-heeled professionals and very-well-heeled professionals. Max Factor III was a classmate, as was Robert "Buzz" Pauley, as in Pauley Petroleum and UCLA's Pauley Pavilion. But in spite of the wealth we were innocent, even by the standards of the time. I did not have one friend whose parents were divorced. I never attended a party at which either drugs or alcohol were present. My most rebellious teenage activities were (1) converting to Christianity for a joke at a Billy Graham rally; (2) smoking cigars in my friend Annette's car; (3) watching a stag film that my friend Rita had found in an alley behind her house. (Like many Beverly Hills residents, Rita's parents owned a projector and she knew how to work it.) Our high school was homogeneous: 100 percent white, about 80 percent Jewish. A reunion of Beverly High students is less a class reunion than a family reunion.

Accompanying the invitation to the reunion was a list of missing persons, those of the 384 classmates who could not be located. I noticed the name of one of my dearest friends from high school, Holly Glickman. Holly stopped speaking to me because I didn't attend her wedding. I always felt guilty about it. There had been many times in the years since when I wanted to talk to Holly, but I felt a special urgency now because something had happened: I had located "The Hedge."

The Hedge was Allan Hedge, a poor unsuspecting fel-

low a year ahead of us with whom Holly and I took a
singing class at Beverly the summer before we were fresh-
men. He first attracted our attention because when each
member of the class had to perform a solo, Allan sang,
"People Will Say We're in Love." This would not have
been noteworthy except that Allan by mistake sang the
girl's part, which began, "Don't throw bouquets at me."
That was enough for us. From then on, "The Hedge," as
we called him, never Allan, became the object of fasci-
nation and ridicule that only two teenagers can create.

I must say in our defense that we never met him, never
even spoke one word to him. He had no way of knowing
that we spent hours rolling on the floor, hysterical with
laughter, talking about him. We wrote the first chapter
of a novel, *The Halls of Beverly,* in which The Hedge was
the hero. He was sort of a cross between a boy and a
beast. We referred to his hands as paws. We made long
lists of book, song, and movie titles, replacing one word
in each title with the word "hedge," as in *Gone With the
Hedge.* We turned a hymn, "Bless This House," into "Bless
This Hedge." One line went, "Bless his rear so firm and
round, it sags so low it 'most touches the ground." The
Hedge did have a somewhat unusual body.

The last Holly or I had heard of The Hedge was one
Christmas vacation during college when Holly claimed to
have spotted him on the beach in Hawaii. (I always thought
this was a hallucination.) But then just before the reunion
invitation arrived, I saw him. I was buying some chopped

meat at a supermarket in Santa Monica and The Hedge was the checker.

I desperately wanted to tell Holly this, just as if we were teenagers again. I even found myself singing "I'm in Love with a Wonderful Hedge" all the way home from the market. (It seems the prospect of this reunion was making me feel a very dopey fifteen.) I knew Holly was a lawyer living in Oakland, and, by calling information, I got a number. But I was hesitant to call. I was afraid that she was still angry and would hang up, even after all these years. I sent her phone number to the reunion committee and hoped they would locate her.

As I wrote my check—$40 for a dinner dance at the Hilton Hotel—I realized that I did not want to attend the reunion alone. At the same time, I did not want Larry to come with me. Mates seem superfluous at events like this. I called Janet Rappaport, class of '62's most likely to succeed.

"A dinner dance at the Hilton!" said Janet, who was now a psychologist, divorced and living in the Bay area. "I'd hate it. I went to my Radcliffe reunion last year and it was really nice. We sat around in small groups and everyone told the truth about how terrible it had been and how bad they felt in comparison to everyone else. Even Iris Brock"—another Beverly classmate who went to Radcliffe—"felt bad, and she's a psychiatrist with a physicist husband, two kids, and a house in Scarsdale. She

has everything!" Janet was only partly joking. "Maybe I
could rent a husband for the night."

"Is that what bothers you?" I said. "Being unattached?"

"No," said Janet. "I have this burden from high school,
being the most likely to succeed. I always felt I didn't
live up to it."

Janet's family was one of the most prestigious in Beverly Hills. Her father, a noted gynecologist, was a prom-
inent member of the local temple. The children were
considered brilliant: Janet was our class valedictorian. But
then, during her first year of college, her father was arrested, accused of performing an illegal abortion. While
this operation could have been considered an act of con-
science—girls needing abortions in those days were usually forced to risk their lives in Tijuana—Beverly Hills
residents found it scandalous. Before he was convicted
(a conviction that was overturned years later), he lost his
Beverly Hills patients. The family sold its large house,
moved to an apartment, and eventually left Beverly Hills
altogether.

Whether from the shock of the event or the accu-
mulated burden of living the perfect life, Janet dropped
out of college for a while. It took her many years—one
commune, one divorce, feminism, a Ph.D., and analysis—
to achieve her present equanimity.

"I don't know," she said, as if she couldn't figure out
why the thought of high school made her feel a failure.
"I love my work. I love my daughter. I love my neigh-

borhood. I have a crush on this totally inappropriate man."

Even without Janet's special burdens, I knew what she meant. Could the facts of anyone's life withstand the judgment of his or her high school peers? I can't think of a less sympathetic group to be judged by. For two weeks, I stared at a questionnaire sent out by the reunion committee. It asked: "Are you married? Do you have children? Honors? Unusual achievements? Rare accomplishments?" There was even this peculiar question: "How many times have you been married?" I couldn't bring myself to fill the questionnaire out.

After talking to a member of the committee who told me that Holly Glickman was still a missing person, I summoned my nerve and called her myself. She was delighted to hear from me.

After a discussion of The Hedge and a certain amount of squealing, Holly said that she would not be caught dead at the reunion but would I please call her afterward and tell her how Toni Lesser is? "I haven't talked to her since we went to college," said Holly. "She was supposed to room with me at Berkeley, but during the summer she got a little wild. She got into trouble, I don't remember why. So her parents punished her. They said, 'You cannot go to Berkeley. You have to go to UCLA and have a nose job.'"

A digression on nose jobs: Almost as if it were tradition, every year several Beverly High students got nose jobs—operations in which their noses were redesigned because they were too large or had an unwanted bump. Girls got them mostly, and occasionally boys, although for them it was less socially acceptable. For some reason nose jobs always took place over Easter vacation, never Thanksgiving or Christmas. One always knew instantly who had had a nose job because the girl returned to school with a little Band-Aid across her nose and two black eyes. She often insisted that she had been forced to have a nose job because of a deviated septum. No one ever believed her.

But although there were many nose jobs, there were only two noses. This was because two Beverly Hills doctors performed virtually all the surgeries, and they were nothing if not consistent. One favored a piglike nose, very turned up; the other, a narrow, bony, scooped-out nose. What these noses had in common was that they never looked like they belonged on the person who sported them. For this reason I always found the face of a girl with a nose job disconcerting. She had normal-looking eyes, a normal-looking mouth, and, in between, a surprise.

Two weeks before the reunion, Janet called. She had decided to come after all and hoped she had enough time to lose five pounds. "You know what everyone does at reunions?" said Janet. "They check out each other's bod."

On the afternoon of the reunion, I got into a slight panic about what to wear and tried on three sweaters. Then I drove to the airport to pick up Janet. The first thing she said was, she couldn't believe it—she had brought the wrong shoes. "We have to go shopping," said Janet. "I can't attend the reunion in these hideous clodhoppers."

On the way to the Hilton Hotel, Janet and I drove past Beverly High. It looked exactly like the Beverly Hills creation it is: rich, pretentious, enviable. Standing on a hill above three perfectly groomed tiers of lawn, the main building is an elegant, sprawling two stories of brick with clock tower and courtyard. French Norman architecture, we were always proudly told. Beverly students are nick-named Normans, and it has always seemed to me a weird Beverly Hills affectation to name students after the archi-tectural style of their school.

As we drove into the hotel parking lot, I was thinking about the things I wanted to find out. How was our class affected by the Vietnam War? Neither Janet nor I knew anyone from our class who went to Vietnam or to Canada or jail to avoid it. Was it possible our entire class of boys was that privileged? I was also interested in how the girls (I can never think of people I went to high school with as anything but boys and girls) were affected by the wom-en's movement. My gut feeling was that our class had spent the last twenty years majoring in analysis and divorce.

As it happened, the idea that I could investigate our class in any systematic way quickly proved absurd. I walked into the room where drinks were being served and was immediately overwhelmed: a sea of faces, each tantalizingly familiar but not identifiable. I felt almost a sense of panic—these people were each connected to some fraction of my past life. It's as though I had three hours to put together a thousand-piece jigsaw puzzle.

My composure was also affected by the fact that, thrust into the midst of my high school classmates, I actually started to feel the way I did in high school. Instantly, involuntarily, I affected a distance, a defense. I was the outsider again. I realized suddenly that what I wanted to "see" at this reunion was not what had happened to my high school friends but what had happened to me. I wanted to return to high school a different person, a person who was now comfortable with herself. But, just my luck, I was not putting my high school identity to rest; instead, it had returned for an encore performance.

I even had a momentary anxiety that no one would talk to me—that I would be, God forbid, a wallflower. This feeling was absolutely in keeping with the past because, although I was not a wallflower, I always believed that with one false move I could become one. As I bought myself a drink, I saw Robert Levin and quickly looked away before he could see me looking. Good grief. I really was fifteen again. I was behaving as though I didn't want Bob Levin to know I had a crush on him.

Bob Levin was my very first boyfriend. I wore his I.D. bracelet for about two weeks when I was eleven. Then he went with Darlene Grob. Then, when we started high school, he took up with Amy Strauss, whom, in my categorical teenage mind, I thought of as very rich, very bland, and very stacked. They never broke up. They were our class's "old married couple," staying together through four years of high school and then marrying during Bob's second year at Dartmouth. Amy and Bob always projected calm, a feeling that was personally unknown to me in adolescence.

In spite of his unavailability and partly because of it, Bob was the most desirable boy in our class. "All-around," as we used to say. Senior class president, good student, varsity football player (though this last was less of a deal at Beverly, which had much better golf and tennis teams than football). Bob was smart but not brilliant, attractive but not gorgeous. That he wasn't extraordinary made him even more desirable: he wasn't threatening.

I never spoke to Bob after age eleven, or, more important, he never spoke to me. I always wished he would. I always thought, If he would just talk to me—just acknowledge my existence—it would confer something special on me. God knows what.

The overwhelming impression in the crowded room was one of prosperity. Everyone was expensively dressed;

also, they were the most well-preserved group one could imagine. That twenty years had passed was less evident from wrinkles than from the fact that many of the men had blow-dried hair. And, if anything, people were thinner than they were in high school. In fact, the talk of the evening turned out to be Earl Fenster. People kept buzzing by and saying, "Have you seen Earl? He's fat!" One fat person in this group caused an uproar. And he wasn't even that fat. It's just that he was very skinny in high school and had grown heavy in an unfortunate manner—it all went to his face, as if his wisdom teeth had been pulled and the swelling never went down.

There was no time to exchange anything but the most superficial pleasantries because as soon as I started one conversation, someone interrupted. We were like bumper cars, crashing into one another, screeching in joy and shock, and then moving on to the next collision. Over and over, my life was reduced to three indexes: marriage, children, career. It felt important to score in all three categories. I scored in two, and just barely, having remarried only that year. I found myself feeling incredibly grateful to my husband, simply because he existed. And to the books I had written for the same reason. They provided me with evidence of a successful life.

The souvenir book had a short description of everyone who returned the questionnaire. The female classmate who seemed to have taken the Beverly Hills life most to heart was described this way: "After years of taking weaving lessons, cooking classes, yoga, piano lessons, aerobic dancing, watercolors, skiing, tennis, and cardiopulmonary resuscitation, Nancy has found true fulfillment as the star of a salad dressing commercial."

My friend Annette LeMot (once a varsity cheerleader, now a ceramic artist) said that everyone seemed really happy, except one person who was described in the book as "divorced and living in Encino." (To Beverly Hills residents, Encino, an area of the San Fernando Valley, is the outback.) Divorced-in-Encino may have been happier than married-and-living-in-Beverly Hills, where at least twenty former classmates still resided. But on this night everyone was judged on externals. In that sense, the reunion was just like high school.

I made a few inquiries. "Do you know anyone who went to Vietnam?" I asked Vince Wyler, now a corporate lawyer in a Los Angeles firm. "Vietnam?" he said. "We went to college." I asked Marty Kaufman, a doctor, how the war affected his life. "I was given the choice of going into the army or into the public health service, working in a pathology laboratory. That's how I became a pathologist." I asked someone else. "I went into the Peace Corps," he said.

Having grown up sheltered, we had found ways to remain so. Lives were eased by inherited money and by successful family businesses to step into. One rumor going around was that a member of the class had been given a shopping center in West Los Angeles for his twenty-first birthday. I bumped into Bob Sinclair, whom everyone still referred to as little Bobby Sinclair because he is short.

"What are you doing?" I said.

"I'm running Sinclair Paints."

At this point the chairman of the reunion committee announced that it was time to eat. We moved into another room, which was decorated in pink and yellow balloons. After an initial flurry of teenage behavior—everyone saving seats—we were served dinner and the socializing continued.

"This is the person I came to see." I looked up. Bob Levin was standing there. Me? I thought. I don't believe it. We started talking as though we were old friends.

Was I married? he asked. I asked where he lived now— Beverly Hills? "No," he said, in a horrified voice, "Brentwood"—as though he had actually moved somewhere. Brentwood, fifteen minutes from Beverly Hills, is one of the poshest areas of West Los Angeles. Of course he had tried to get his kids into the Beverly Hills schools but there was no legal way to do it. He told me that he was a lawyer, that he and Amy had four children, a fifth was on the way. I looked at him. He was handsomer, thinner of course, as decent as ever. I asked him how he and Amy managed to make a lifelong commitment based on their high school identities. He said only, "Amy and I have an extraordinary relationship."

All this was infuriating. My fantasy of a reunion was that the creeps turned out handsome and the popular kids peaked at age eighteen. But Bob marched on. Like a Beverly Hills house, he had just grown more valuable.

It was difficult for me to concentrate on what Bob was saying, partly because I was overwhelmed, partly because I was confused. I didn't know why he had sought me out. I assumed it was because I had had some public success. But that may not have been the reason. He didn't ask about my writing. He mentioned that I was his first girlfriend. True, and that's sweet. And since he'd only had three in his whole life, maybe it was a big deal. He even suggested that we had something in common. I had no idea what. Could it be that I drooled over him in high school? He couldn't possibly have known that.

What could we have in common? Me with my divorce and five years of psychotherapy. Me, who didn't write seriously until I was thirty-one and didn't really fall in love until I was thirty-five. Life had been so easy for Bob. Or maybe it just looked that way, and I, like everyone else, was judging by externals. All I knew for sure was I was fifteen years old again, and the boy I had a crush on was talking to me.

After Bob hugged me, I sat down. Both Janet and Annette said, practically in unison, practically squealing, "What did he say? What did he say?"

Before I had time to answer, someone in this crowd of 1962 graduates started yelling. It was not clear what he was yelling. It was only clear immediately that he was crazy. A strange quiet descended on the room, everyone craning his neck to see who was making the disturbance. It was a tall, bald man. Some speculated that he was from our class, but because of his bald head they couldn't place him. Others insisted he was a gate-crasher, bringing the real world into Beverly Hills, where it had no business. Two hotel security guards were brought in to deal with the problem, which meant there were now two black people at the reunion. More real world. The man was subdued but not removed. He remained seated for the rest of the festivities, and people steered clear.

At eleven-thirty, the reunion was over. I didn't want to leave, though I had said hello to everyone I wanted to say hello to. But there was something I didn't want to lose. Possibly it was the present. That night I had described my life at thirty-seven so many times, so superficially, so glibly, that even I had begun to believe my life had no warts. Possibly it was the past—the teenager I was, back for one night only. I had more affection for her now.

It was naive of me to imagine I could return to high school a different person. Coming from a family of many siblings, I know how difficult it is to shake a role—a label that parents and relatives affix to keep the kids differentiated: she's the bright one, the jock, the pretty one. I always imagine that I will return—to some reunion, some Thanksgiving dinner—and not only will I not feel like the child I once was, but everyone will see who I truly am. When the event is over, having survived seems quite enough.

"Well," said Janet, "that's it till the thirtieth."

"The thirtieth?" someone behind me said. "That's when the years are really going to show."

Maybe. In Beverly Hills, I wouldn't bet on it.

The Art Lesson

A few years after my husband married for the first time, a friend who had recently decided to become an artist gave him and his wife one of his works of art. It arrived in a small cardboard box sealed with masking tape. Larry opened it and found an oval-shaped mound of orange hair. The oval was about eight inches across; the mound was matted like a bird's nest; the hair was fake, like acrylic. Because it was a gift, Larry felt he should display it though he was not sure how. He asked the artist, who said to hang it. So Larry put some tape on the back and stuck it to the wall. It looked quite odd, like an insect habitat that wouldn't exist if your home had been properly fumigated. After a few weeks and several stupefied visitors, Larry removed the piece, returned it to the cardboard box, which he had thoughtfully saved, and put it in the closet.

Twelve years later. Larry is now separated. One day when he returns the children after a weekend at his place, his ex-wife greets him at the door with his share of their belongings: his mother's teacups, some record albums, and the cardboard box.

"Do you think we should hang this?" He shows me the mashed-looking bird's nest.

"Why would we want to do that?"

"Craig Aronson made it. He's getting kind of successful now."

I have not met Craig Aronson but I know who he is. He's the ex-husband of the woman who introduced Larry and me. "That's the worst-looking thing I've ever seen," I say.

"Yeah, I know," says Larry. He puts it back in the box and puts the box in the closet.

Four years later. Larry's friend Victor calls from New York City. He mentions that he has just been to a fantastic gallery show of an artist named Craig Aronson.

"Oh, I have a piece of his," says Larry. "A really early one, a sort of sculpture."

"Are you kidding?" says Victor. "At this show small drawings the size of a Kleenex are selling for twelve thousand dollars. That piece is worth, minimum, fifteen thousand. You've got to get it appraised."

Larry hangs up. In a panic he checks the closet to make sure the piece is still there.

After we spend an hour discussing what we would do with an extra fifteen thousand dollars, we spend fifteen minutes discussing some ramifications of owning a possibly valuable work of art after two divorces, the artist's and one's own. To wit: The artist's ex-wife got custody of the friendship with Larry and his then wife, Ellen. As a result, Larry and Craig have not been in touch in ten years. Since the piece is not signed, Larry has to write Craig for authentication. This is (1) awkward and (2) tricky—suppose Craig realizes Larry wants to sell the piece? Will he be insulted? Furthermore, Larry's ex-wife may not know what she gave away when she handed him the box (not to mention that it might be valuable). Had she looked inside or was she just handing over the contents of his office closet? We decide that Larry should eventually write Craig and never mention anything about this to Ellen.

At this point Lisa comes into the room. "What's that?" she says, horrified, pointing to the possibly valuable piece sitting on the coffee table.

Not that Lisa has her finger on the pulse of the art world, but her reaction does bring me back to earth. "We're being crazy," I say. "Nobody is going to want this thing."

"But it's a Craig Aronson," says Larry.

I think about this. What for years has been a thing is now a Craig Aronson. I try to imagine it in an art gallery. Already I'm in trouble because I can't imagine how it's hung. Not possibly by masking tape. I decide it's suspended from wire. A woman walks in. "I've got to have that," she says. No, too rash. "That piece is interesting," she says. "Let me take it home and see how it wears." That makes more sense—not love at first sight but an attraction. Unfortunately my fantasy falls apart when I try to imagine her showing the piece to her husband. How could his response be anything but confusion? She went into a gallery and came out with this? Well, erase the husband. Maybe the lady lives alone. Like everyone else connected with this work of art, she's divorced. And going blind.

I try another fantasy. In this one I am carrying the cardboard box into Sotheby's. The appraiser opens it and lifts out the mound. He examines it. He looks at me strangely. He speaks—

No, I speak. "You'd better be the one to have this appraised," I say to Larry. "I'd be too embarrassed."

A week later. Victor calls. "Did you do it?"

"Not yet," says Larry.

"Come on, it's worth a fortune. You can't imagine how hot this guy is."

That night three friends come to dinner. We tell them about the piece, how awful we think it is, that we're even too embarrassed to have it appraised. We also mention that drawings by Craig Aronson the size of a Kleenex are selling for twelve thousand dollars.

Our dinner guests have not been keeping up with the

New York art world, so they have not heard of Craig
Aronson. Still, they are skeptical. Either he's not famous,
they say, or the piece is not terrible. They've seen lots
of peculiar examples of modern art—reproductions of
stop signs, collages of toilet seats. We take out the box
and show them the piece. All three collapse into hysterical
laughter. I feel vindicated.

Three days later. There is a message on our phone
machine from Robby, one of our dinner guests. "Call me.
It's about your Craig Aronson."

Robby reports that he had lunch that day with a curator
from the Los Angeles Museum of Contemporary Art.
Just to see if we knew what we were talking about, he
mentioned that his friends have a sculpture by Craig
Aronson, and she flipped: He's one of the most interesting artists working today; she has to see the piece;
would we bring it down? does he think we'd donate it?—
we could get a tax deduction.

"I'm not sure you want it," Robby said to her.

"I want it," she said.

"It's kind of strange."

"I don't care."

"But it looks like a very large orange Brillo pad."

"Hmmm," said the curator. "I'm not familiar with that
period of his work."

Robby says to call her right away—everything by a
famous artist is worth something, even this.

Two weeks later. August 1984. We have an appointment with the curator. On the way, I have two fantasies. In one she is stunned, enchanted by the piece. In the other she is just stunned. I know which fantasy is more likely to occur, but I don't know which I prefer. Do I want my taste validated or a tax deduction?

The curator takes us into her office. Larry places the cardboard box in the center of her desk. We chat a few minutes, nobody making a move toward the box. Finally Larry says, "Why don't you open it?" Slowly she pulls up the top and looks in. Silence. "Feel free to take it out," says Larry.

Very gently she lifts the mound out of the box. "Oh, my," she says. Then she stares at it awhile in silence. "What's it made of?"

"We're not sure," says Larry.

The curator holds the mound against the wall. It does not improve. Another silence.

"Robby said everything by a famous artist is worth something," I say.

She says, "Everything by a famous artist is not worth something."

She pulls a Whitney Museum catalog of Craig Aronson's work off a shelf and quickly thumbs through. She finds nothing resembling the piece. "Maybe it's part of his juvenilia," says Larry, a little depressed. She laughs.

"Come on," I say, feeling chummy, thinking I have detected that she shares my opinion of this piece. "If you didn't know this was by a well-known artist, would you ever think it was, or that he had talent?"

"That's the question, isn't it?" she says, not answering it. We chat a few more minutes about how Larry happens to know Craig Aronson, while the piece sits there, looking as if it might crawl off the desk of its own accord. Then, as we are about to put it back in the box, she asks if she can hold on to it and show it to the museum director when he returns from his vacation. We say okay. She shows us out.

As we get in the car, Larry says, "What are we going to do with it if she doesn't want it? I don't feel right selling it."

"Of course she doesn't want it."

"She didn't say that."

He's right. I was so intent on my point of view, I didn't notice. "We could throw it away."

"We can't throw it away," says Larry. "It's art."

A month later. The curator has not returned Larry's many phone calls and we are beginning to get outraged— we want our Craig Aronson back. Finally, one evening she calls. She has shown the piece to the museum director and he is, as she puts it, "as baffled by it as I am." Still, she says, they do not want to give it back. They have contacted Craig and are sending him a Polaroid of it. They want to hear what he has to say.

A week later. Victor calls. In the Craig Aronson Whitney catalog he has found a photograph of a sculpture that looks similar to ours. Larry repeats to me what it says: " 'Untitled, 1968, Dyed Nylon Monofilament. Destroyed.' "

"Is that an order from the artist? That we should destroy it if we have it?"

"Not destroy," says Larry. " 'Destroyed.' It probably means we have something rare."

He phones the curator to tell her of his discovery, but she does not return his call. Now I have another fantasy. The museum does not want the piece but loses it. We declare a loss. My taste is validated *and* we get a tax deduction. Then I have one more fantasy. Ellen, Larry's ex, hears of the museum's vague interest from one of the seventeen people that I have sworn to secrecy about it. She takes him back to court for her share of the piece and, while she's at it, ups the alimony and child support. We have to sell our house and move south of Venice Boulevard, where I will get mugged.

Three months later. December 1984. The curator phones. Craig Aronson has identified the piece as one of a series done in 1968 of which only three or four remain. "While we were somewhat amused by the piece originally, we have come to think of it as wonderful and original," she says. "We would like to have it for our permanent collection." She adds that they plan to hang it in the show that opens their permanent museum in December 1986.

"How are you going to hang it?" says Larry, thinking

he can finally get the answer to something that has been troubling him for years.

"I don't know," she says. "Craig will be here, and I'm sure he'll have some ideas."

Then the kicker. In the catalog of their permanent collection, they are going to say how they came by each piece. They consider our story the most charming—as the curator put it, "the way you came in with that little box."

Larry and she talk a few more minutes. He asks her if she will appraise the work for him. She says, No, no one at the museum can—it's a conflict of interest. He should contact Heidi Cole, whose New York City gallery sells Aronson's work. Then she says there is a big museum show opening tomorrow, black tie, and it's too late to send us an invitation but she would be happy to leave our names at the door. Larry declines. They say good-bye. He hangs up and immediately calls Victor. Victor says, "If they want the piece so much, why don't they buy it?"

I call the three people who saw the work when they had dinner at our house. They say it's unbelievable.

Larry calls Heidi Cole, who does not take his call.

Four months later. After several periodic attempts, Larry reaches Heidi Cole, it seems because Craig Aronson happens to be in the gallery at the moment Larry phones and identifies him as a friend. She says there are problems. Normally when she appraises something, she prices it according to what a similar piece has sold for. But no piece like this of Craig Aronson's has ever been sold. Furthermore, she is a member of an art dealers' alliance so she can't appraise the work through the gallery. Larry must submit the piece to the alliance and, for a couple of hundred dollars, the alliance will appraise it, though she is not sure how.

Larry does not want to spend a couple of hundred dollars. He appeals to Craig Aronson directly.

Craig, having heard of the impending donation to the museum, is delighted to help. He will attempt to prevail upon Heidi Cole to write a letter indicating, for insurance purposes, what the piece is worth. Then he estimates, tops, it's worth $5,000.

Larry hangs up. "Why give away a work of art for that?" he says.

"Are you kidding?" I say. "Take the deduction."

"No," says Larry. "Maybe he'll get really famous and it will be worth a lot more. I'll give it to the museum on permanent loan." He writes the curator.

Four months later. A letter arrives from the museum. We completely understand the position you are in and feel that at this point it would be best for us to return the work to you with our great thanks and best wishes. Leaving the piece here at the museum on loan would not be workable for us because there is not an appropriate context in which to show it at this time. Our registrar will be in touch with you regarding return of the work to you.

A month later. The doorbell rings and a young woman hands Larry a small cardboard box. He checks to make sure the piece is in it and puts it in the closet.

Delia's Laws

I have a theory that a quarter of what I buy turns out to be a mistake. In my closet, there are always a couple of brand-new, six-month-old pairs of shoes sitting in their boxes (at this moment, pointy-toed white flats and glad-iator sandals). There are always several once-worn items of clothing—currently, among others, a turquoise silk blouse and matching skirt (yes, I was invited to a wedding; no, I was not the mother of the bride). There is an olive green wallet which I use but hate, $240 worth of glass drawer handles (this is too complicated to explain), and eight flower-print napkins that have never been taken out of their box. There have been more expensive errors as well. Namely one Fiat Strada, a rather large compact car whose color could charitably be described as pumpkin, and whose design could most flatteringly be described as boxy. It looked like a car in a Richard Scarry children's book. A rabbit should have driven it; not I, who was forced to for three years (cars cannot exactly be consigned to the closet), until it was demolished in an accident from which I escaped with a small bump on my head.

Oddly enough, these mistakes have occurred whether I agonized over a purchase or bought rashly. Which brings me to another theory I have, a sort of corollary to the first: There is no way to know which purchases will be busts until it is too late to return them. In the case of the Fiat, it was about thirty seconds after driving out of the car dealership.

The reason I have theories about shopping is that I have theories about everything. I share this tendency to sum up with my mother, who was inclined less to converse than to make pronouncements. She was a sort of maternal Aesop who dispensed with the story and moved right on to the moral. "Mom, I'm upset. Richie broke up with me." Mom: "Never marry a man with fat ankles." Her logic was difficult to follow, being at best elliptical, at worst nonexistent. For instance, Richie and I were not even considering getting married—I was about sixteen. After some prodding I discovered that "never marry a man with fat ankles" was a reference to the fact that my mother didn't want me to have children with fat ankles. So she was saying, in effect, that given the size of Richie's ankles, I was better off without him.

I always thought theorizing was my mother's way of being motherly. With these maxims, she could pass on to me what she knew and still maintain a distance that was comfortable for her. But now that I am a major theorizer myself, I think something more was going on. I think theorizing is an attempt to get the upper hand on life.

For me, the scariest thing about life is the possibility of an accident. I hate it that we are all potential victims of the freak event, under which umbrella I include a momentary lapse of taste in a car showroom and a flowerpot falling on one's head. I include mental lapses among the accidental because I, at least, seem to have about as much control upstairs, so to speak, as on the street. I always find myself conducting post-mortems on my seemingly inexplicable behavior. Why did I do that? Why did I say that? What was I thinking? I should have known better. I deal with the unpredictableness of life quite sensibly: by trying to deny it. I am always making up some rule, some after-the-fact law, to account for why something unexpected has occurred. My theories give me the illusion that the unexpected was, if not expectable, at least explicable. They make life neater and, especially, safer.

Of course, since I am my mother's daughter, my theories tend to the illogical. And since they are more for comfort than guidance, they are sometimes only applicable in hindsight. Perhaps for this reason, though I am always theorizing, I can only remember these twelve rules.

1. You can never afford to buy a house.
2. Never have anything done to your house that you couldn't stand to have done twice.
3. Never buy a speckled carpet.
4. Anything wrong with a house can cause a fight between two people living in it.
5. Always buy jeans that are too tight for you.
6. Never hire a doctor who's younger than you.
7. One quarter of what you buy will turn out to be mistakes.
8. Nine tenths of the people you fall in love with will turn out to be mistakes.
9. Someone will always tell you what you want to hear.
10. Never judge anyone by his or her ex.
11. The distance from your friend's house to the airport is always ten minutes farther than your friend says it is.
12. When you return from a trip, the time it takes to feel you need a vacation is the time between opening your front door and listening to your telephone messages.

I Am the
Green Lollipop:
Notes on Stepmothering

Lisa and Alex, ages six and three, were standing in a fountain in the middle of the Santa Monica Mall. I insisted they get out. They refused. Again I insisted. Lisa put her arm around her brother and drew him closer to her.

This is what happened the first time I was left alone with my future stepchildren. I insisted they get out of a fountain that did not have water in it. I have given this act of mine considerable thought. At the very least, it indicates a certain amount of panic on my part. A tendency to overreact. Certainly a lack of playfulness. I could have gotten into the fountain with them. I also could have ignored the whole business, waited for their father to return, and let him deal with it or not. But I couldn't wait. I had to seize an opportunity, any opportunity, to assert my authority.

My claim to authority at that time was tenuous—I was not yet their stepmother. I must have wanted to prove just how tenuous it was. Why else would I try to stop two children from doing nothing? Naturally they refused to obey me. But more was at stake here and we all knew it—our futures. Lisa and Alex were seizing an opportunity themselves: They were taking a stand against me, the intruder. It is one of the few moments in their lives when they have been in agreement. And I, in my muddleheaded way, continued to insist, "Get out," when what I really meant was, "Let me in."

Lisa wanted a horse desperately. She had been talking about it for weeks and then said she would give up Christmas for three years to get one.

Larry said, "Lisa, I don't think you realize, it's very expensive, not just to buy a horse but to keep a horse. It costs several thousand dollars a year."

"My friends will give me the food free," said Lisa.

"Lisa, that's impossible," said Larry, exasperated. "We can't afford a horse."

Lisa stomped up the stairs, then halfway up yelled, very sarcastically, "Thanks, Delia."

I would like to point out that I had not said one word.

It doesn't matter. I am the cause of her pain, whatever it may be, perhaps because she blames me for her much greater hurt, that her parents are no longer married. I am not the reason they are divorced, but I am evidence of it, as well as being a hindrance. How can they get back together if I'm here? I am also privileged to be the adult that Lisa can most risk being angry with or, put another way, that she can most afford to have angry with her. Life is less secure than it used to be and she isn't taking any chances. So when Lisa feels mistreated, she thinks of me.

The only problem with her point of view from my point of view is this: How can I be her persecutor if I'm her victim? For I *am* her victim. My identity as a stepmother is amorphous at best, and if she takes this away from me, what will I have left? Consider:

Larry and his first wife got divorced. Both stayed involved with their children so Lisa now has two mothers—two mothers because she has her regular mother and she has her father. Now that he sees the children alone, Larry is doing a lot of mothering—feeding, soothing, bathing, reading, setting limits (well, sort of—more on this later). Then I arrive and suddenly Lisa has three mothers.

Two were difficult enough. Lisa is in the peculiar position of being overloaded with mothers and deprived of family. And she is possessive and protective of her father, feeling vulnerable to losing him altogether now that the family has fallen apart. And how do I fit in? Who am I, as far as Lisa is concerned? Unwelcome and unnecessary.

Unfortunately for her, I am also unstoppable—though that won't keep her from trying.

When I first arrived, I checked out the territory. I wanted to participate. I wanted to be helpful. Well, truthfully, I wanted most to become indispensable. To Larry, not to Lisa, who, at least in the beginning, was simply a means to an end. So what did I seize upon? Cooking and chauffeuring. (And one other task—criticizing—but we'll get to that later.)

Even if I had known I was cooking my own goose, I would have taken on these jobs; they were the only ones available. The problem that developed was this: When I cooked my own goose, Lisa wouldn't eat it. Because I can cook all I want, but I can't feed. Feeding is what mothers do, and here Lisa drew the line. "I'm not hungry," she said, or something equally upsetting, like, "I just feel like eating yogurt tonight." It was her way of saying, "You can't mother me." So, at least in part, my efforts were thwarted. I was getting little payoff for my hard work. Though I succeeded in becoming indispensable to Larry, I wasn't satisfied. I wanted love. Lisa's love. I wanted this even before I loved Lisa myself, for its symbolic meaning—that I belonged in the family. Oh, what an unreasonable expectation. The self-centeredness of it. Of course, I might have settled for gratitude or respect, but good luck to me.

So the inevitable took place. I began to feel used. The rest of the world may see me as a wicked stepmother, but I see myself as Cinderella in a fairy tale that goes something like this: Once upon a time, there was a handsome prince who fell in love with a beautiful princess (me). He took her away to his castle to live with him and his two children from a previous marriage. Here things quickly went to pot, and the princess became known, at least to herself, as Cinderella. Now she could have given up cooking and driving the coach-and-four, but then she wouldn't have been Cinderella. And what would she be?

A problem, you see, of options.

It happens, however, that there is another role, besides that of victim, that is available to me: the outsider. The problem is, Lisa has a stake in this identity too. She feels driven out by my relationship with her father, while I feel doomed never to be allowed full membership in the club. It occurs to me that one of the unappreciated side effects of all this uncoupling and recoupling is the endless opportunity it offers all participants to feel sorry for themselves. I was at the door of our house one day having a conversation with my husband's ex-wife. She complained about having to miss *The Jewel in the Crown* on television that night. I said we were going to miss it too. "Oh, but you can tape it," she said. "Why don't you?" I asked, falling into the trap. "I don't have a tape machine," she said mournfully.

This conversation wasn't about a television show. She was actually saying, You have more money than me; life is so much harder for me; I am the victim. Well, let me say this about that: Hands off my role!

How to Talk to Your Stepmother

Your stepmother answers the telephone.
"Hi, is my dad there?"

Your stepmother has just announced that it's time for dinner.
"I'm not hungry."

Your stepmother has just put a bottle of salad dressing on the table.
"This isn't the kind we have at Mom's."

Your stepmother has just put the chicken on the table.
"I don't like chicken in funny sauce."

Your dad, your stepmother, and you are going to the movies. You don't want to see the movie she wants to see.
"My mom says that movie is too violent for me."
Alternatives
    1. "My mom says that movie is too scary."
    2. "My mom says that movie is too sad."

You want to watch television. Your stepmother says no.
"I'll ask my dad."

You ask your dad if you can watch television. Your step-mother informs him that she already told you you can't.
"I'm not talking to you. I'm talking to my dad!"

Your dad is out in the afternoon and you turn on the television. Your stepmother says to turn it off.
"You're not the boss of me."

You want your stepmother to take you to a movie that she thinks your dad doesn't want you to see.
"Look, you're my stepmother. You're in charge. You don't have to ask him."

Your stepmother picks up you and your friend after the movies.
"Hi, where's Dad? Why didn't he come?"

Your dad says you are not allowed to sleep over at your friend's. Absolutely not. It's out of the question. Tomorrow's a school day. Your stepmother says nothing.
"That was your idea, wasn't it?"

Lisa, pleading, was following Larry from room to room. She'd never be rude again, she promised, if he would please, please, please, take the punishment back and let her have dessert. I listened. Would he change his mind? Would he? "If I see good behavior for the rest of the day, you can have some ice cream after dinner," said Larry. Lisa danced off. I was outraged.

This scenario takes place with some frequency. The subject varies: Lisa wants to stay up an hour later than the bedtime Larry has set for her; she wants one more cookie than the number he has given her. Whatever. The constants are these: She wants him to change his mind; I listen, convinced, even panicked, that he will; and then, he does.

This brings me to the stepmother's most important function from her point of view, and her most dispensable from everyone else's: criticizing. Though she would describe it as "seeing things clearly."

Because she is a stepmother and, again her words, "not involved," she can't help notice her husband's little failures as a father. Naturally she is nearly driven crazy by what she sees. Oh, the frustration of it, having to stand by and just watch. Of course, she wants to be helpful. So she points out to her husband how he is "letting his child down" and expects him to shape up.

"It's not good for Lisa to have a daddy who reneges on the limits he has set," I say to Larry the second Lisa leaves the room, and sometimes before, which drives Lisa mad. "It's not your business!" she screams at me. But doesn't she understand? It's my duty to interfere, for her sake.

I am utterly convinced that, were I this child's mother, I would never change my mind once it was made up. (Since I am not the child's mother, I am safe from ever finding out I'm wrong.) I regularly compliment myself with the thought, I'm much tougher than Larry is, and when given the opportunity I always prove I am. (Of course, I am—I'm the stepmother and not involved.) Right is on my side. Parents should set limits and stick to them—all psychologists agree with me. My friends all sympathize with my uphill struggle to whip my husband into shape. They know all about it because I complain to them regularly—"Why doesn't he see what he's doing?" It doesn't temper my zealousness or make me more understanding to know that many divorced fathers are too indulgent, and there are reasons for it. I even know the reasons. They feel guilty about the divorce and are continually trying to make it up to their children by being nice. They are worried about losing their children's love, though, as all of us who read the psychology books know, children interpret limits as love. (Even when the daddies know this, their anxiety may make them unable to act on it.) And possibly some other reasons as well: laziness—it's easier to be nice than tough; misplaced generosity—the feeling that limiting your child is in some way being stingy; and inexperience as a disciplinarian. Being reluctant or too insecure to discipline your child is a sad situation to be in, but I am not saddened by it because I am too busy trying to do something about it.

Larry always listens patiently to my pleas. He agrees with me. He's letting his daughter down. He must change. He will learn to be tougher. But why can't I shut up about it?

Why can't I? No parent wants an unbiased observer in the house watching him. That is truly a parent's night-mare—at the least he should be allowed to screw up in private. And no one but a stepmother would think that a stepmother is unbiased. This is the tricky part. I may be right, but my motives are not what they seem.

To be as honest as possible, I sense not that I can't help but notice my husband's failings, but that a little part of me lies in wait for them. Is he going to change his mind? He does and I pounce. And behind all my helpful criticism is a needling, an implied "If you won't follow my advice, who knows what will happen to your daughter!" I stir Larry up a little. It's a way of getting back at him for the fact that I'm not involved. Because despite what-ever special perception the outside position gives me, I resent being there. In other words, I am an unbiased observer with a grudge.

Oh, dear. I suppose it sounds dreadful to be married to me. My husband probably deserves condolences. But, please, consider my frustration. Lisa and Alex live with us three days a week. Their behavior affects me yet I can do little to affect their behavior. My hands are not tied, but appropriately the main disciplining is done by Larry. It's as though I'm standing in a rainstorm and, to keep dry, I have to convince Larry to open an umbrella. If he doesn't mind the wet, then I get wet too.

And another thing. I have no vote in the larger deci-sions made about Lisa and Alex, though naturally I have much to contribute on this score. Let's say Alex has to change schools, and his mother is doing the initial screening. I tell Larry about some schools that might be right. If he agrees with me, then he has to believe my suggestions are important enough to present to his ex. Here we run into a slight difference of opinion. He thinks only certain things are worth taking up with his ex; I think almost everything is because I was not married to her. In any event, presuming he conveys my opinion (as his, of course, because she is not interested in mine, and frankly, in her spot, I wouldn't be either), the question then becomes, Will she act on it? Guess what the chances are.

Blocked on all fronts, I occasionally get desperate. If Lisa is begging Larry to commute her sentence, I butt in before he has a chance to answer. "Your father doesn't change his mind," I say, which, aside from being untrue, doesn't give Larry much choice. It occurs to me that when I complain to my friends, "Why can't he see what he's doing?" perhaps I am really saying, "Why can't he do what I tell him?" I must be reacting to my lack of power. I mean, overreacting. That's the kindest excuse I can think of.

Quotes from Stepchildren (not mine)

"A stepmother is not a mother. She can help you with your homework and make dinner, but she should not be able to decide when you should go to bed. If you have a fight with your dad, your stepmother should stay out of it. You can complain to your stepmom about your mom, but your stepmom should not complain about your mom to you because it's none of her business and she doesn't even know her."

"The title stepmother has absolutely no meaning except that it means she's married to my father. She's another adult. Sort of a friend, but not exactly."

"A stepmother should be supportive. I don't think she should actively participate unless she has to. Not a mother or a father. She should know her place."

Lisa and Alex were leaving for camp. We were at the bus. All of us: the children, their father, their mother, and me. It was the perfect picture of the 1980s family—three parents seeing two children off to camp. Larry was making sure the kids had pre-stamped and -addressed envelopes so they would write. Their mother was hunting for the camp nurse to give her Alex's antibiotic. I stood there holding a package of M&M's for each, thinking, I'm going to be kissed goodbye last.

It crosses my mind, as I write this, what a pathetic, whiny little thought that was. My husband and his ex-wife were getting on with the business of parenting, and I was thinking about me. How much am I loved? And, assessing the situation accurately, I concluded, "Less."

Of course, less. Less is appropriate. So why was I standing there reminding myself, feeling yet again sorry for myself? It happens I had nothing else to do. Once again I am undone by my extraneousness. But the problem goes deeper. Back to childhood even.

I have three sisters. I am the second oldest, a middle child. When I was growing up, I had four stuffed animals—I'll spare you their names—and every night I slept with a different one. Always in the same order, rotating one night for each. I concluded, looking back years later, that the animals represented my three sisters and me, and I was playing Mommy, doling out the affection in equal parts. I must have been worried about getting as much love as my sisters, perhaps because I lacked the distinction of being the oldest or the youngest. To reassure myself, I played this game.

And now, thirty years later, I found myself standing in a YMCA parking lot, thinking, I'm going to be kissed goodbye last. At this moment I was a child again. I had turned my husband and his ex-wife into siblings, and we were all vying for the love of our parents, Lisa and Alex. This time I was getting what I always feared—the short end.

As a stepmother, I am vulnerable to these psychic attacks of regression for one reason: I'm not a parent.

In your standard-issue family—of which few remain, but on which our expectations are still based—there are parents and there are children. The way you know which are which, aside from certain size and age differences and despite any behavior similarities, is that the parents are the bossy ones. When necessary, they get to tell the children what to do. It's their right, and it's how they exercise responsibility for their children's welfare. The process of growing up is one in which the child chips away at the parents' right to boss—i.e., control—and assumes more and more responsibility.

The dilemma the stepmother finds herself in is she doesn't have the right to boss. This is not simply a source of frustration but an even more serious problem of not being franchised. "A stepmother can help you with your homework, but she should not be able to decide when you should go to bed." That stepchild was saying that a stepmother can do things parents do, but she is not a parent. Much as I would like to beg the issue and say, possibly childishly, "I can too tell my stepkids when to go to bed," the truth is I have this right only in the absence of Larry or with his tacit permission. Permission, even tacit, is not something parents need, it's something children need.

One Sunday morning, I got into a disagreement with Lisa over our family's trip to the flea market. I wanted to get there early and she wanted us all to wait two hours until her friend could come too. I found myself making my case to Larry as she made hers. Crammed in his walk-in closet as he put on his shirt were Lisa and I, both asking Daddy for permission.

This situation alone could make me feel like a child. But in fact, as a stepmother, I am a child anyway. By default. Because in a family, if you aren't a parent, what are you?

I would like to mention, apropos of that incident in the closet, that Larry thought his predicament was the worst because he was caught in the middle between his daughter and me. Larry: I'm the victim. Delia: I'm the victim. Lisa: *I'm* the victim. But despite evidence to the contrary, my battle has not been for victim-of-the-family award. My battle has been, not to sound too arch, more with myself. I don't want to feel like a child in this marriage. I want to be an adult around these children, even though I am not their parent. I may have failed occasionally, as in fighting for the right to go to the flea market my way, but I have been pretty successful coping with my childish fantasies. At least I keep quiet about them.

I don't mean I keep my little deprived feelings hidden, guarding them as though they are the precious threads of an insecurity blanket. I mean I dismiss them as one of the hazards of having a title with no job to go with it. When that stepchild I talked to said, "A stepmother should know her place," he did not understand that her place is not known. I am from moment to moment mother, father, aunt, maid, sibling—borrowing behavior from each but having none that is exclusively or legitimately mine. Being rootless, I can't be faulted for indulging in some childish daydreams. But, think what I may, I always kiss my step-kids goodbye last, gracefully, and don't dwell on the unfairness of it. Everyone knows life is unfair. Besides, there will always be other opportunities to feel unloved. Soon. Like when my stepchildren write letters home from camp and the salutations read, "Dear Dad."

A Stepmother's Fantasies

My stepchildren will go into analysis and spend the entire time discussing how much they hate me.

My stepchildren will be in analysis five days a week for five years and never mention me once.

I will have to pay for my stepchildren's analysis.

My husband will die, and his ex-wife will get all his money.

I will die, and his ex-wife will get all my money.

My husband will die, and I'll never see my stepchildren again.

My husband will die, his ex will die, and I'll end up with them.

Larry, Lisa, Alex, and I went out for hamburgers. We were shown to a booth that seats two on one side, two on the other. "I'm sitting with Dad!" both kids shouted and threw themselves into the seat next to him. I sat down on the other side, which meant there were now three squeezed into one side and one alone (me) on the other.

Naturally, I felt a little rejected. Naturally, I felt completely ridiculous for feeling rejected. I mean, really! So instantly, almost reflexively, I covered. I didn't exactly smile as though I were amused by the children's behavior, but I tried to affect a facial expression that indicated I was perfectly happy sitting alone. Perfectly happy, as they piled their coats on my side because I had more room. But then I started worrying that people in the restaurant were watching. I felt like a teenager caught publicly in an embarrassing situation. I felt even more ridiculous for feeling embarrassed. I reminded myself that I was a grown-up. Embarrassment was not appropriate here. Once again I was having a problem keeping a firm grip on my adulthood.

I studied the menu while Larry said, "It's impossible to eat sitting this crowded," and Lisa and Alex began arguing about who had to move. "I got here first!" they both claimed. I ignored them. Then Lisa said, "Alex, it is so mean of you to leave Delia sitting all alone there." Alex said, "Well, why do I have to be the one?" Larry said, "Look, you kids sit together. I'm sitting with Delia."

"No!" They threw themselves against him.

At that moment, listening to Lisa and Alex fight over who got to sit with their father or, put another way, who had to sit with me, I finally realized what my place in the family is. I am the green lollipop. (Larry is the red one.) In other words, in the battle between the siblings, whoever gets me loses.

Lisa wanted her dad to take her to the movies, but he couldn't—he had to work.

"I'll take you," I said.

"Hey, great," said Lisa. As she walked out of the room, I heard her say to herself, almost surprised, "That's one good thing about having a stepmother." I sighed but reminded myself that being useful is better than being extraneous. I also wished that Lisa would have the decency to keep some thoughts to herself.

A few moments later, I got a telephone call that my close friend's mother had died and she wanted me to attend the funeral. I would have to leave for New York City that afternoon. Listening to me talk on the phone, Lisa burst into tears. "Oh, Lisa," I said, "I'm really sorry I can't take you to the movies."

"That's not why I'm crying," she sobbed. "I don't want you to go," and she threw herself into my arms.

Which brings me to the subject of ambivalence. Between marriages, I had many boyfriends cursed with this trait. One used to say, when I complained about his emotional unpredictability, "It's not me, it's my ambivalence," as though his ambivalence were an untamed pet that kept messing on the carpet. Along with New York City, ambivalence was something I left behind when I met Larry. Or so I thought. Until I met Lisa.

It is inevitable that Lisa would be ambivalent about her stepmother. One of my defenses against taking her see-sawing emotions too seriously is to say that I personally am totally lovable; it's my title that causes the problem. But, actually, her ambivalence does not entirely have to do with me or my title but is general fallout from the divorce.

When I talk to children whose parents are divorced, I am very struck by something I hear again and again. As if reciting a memorized poem, they repeat what their parents said when they separated: "Parents may get divorced, but they never divorce their children." Or "Mommy and Daddy may stop loving each other, but they always love their children." Any child who is given this line will believe it on the one hand—it's what Mommy and Daddy said—and doubt it on the other. They have to doubt it, at least subconsciously, because it doesn't make sense. If Mommy and Daddy can stop loving each other, they can stop loving their children. Let's be honest. Let's be logical. Besides, all these kids have friends whose parents have been divorced. And in some of the cases, one of those parents took off, never to be heard from again, or rarely. Lisa and Alex each have a friend to whom that has happened.

It's understandable why parents say these things, even

if they're not true. They are desperate to comfort their children. They want the divorce to be all right for their kids because it is right for them. I imagine that many of these enlightened parents have told their friends, "It's not good for children to have parents who don't love each other." That's true. It just doesn't follow that it's necessarily better for these children if their parents divorce. I'm not arguing that people shouldn't get divorced. I can't bear to think of what my life would be like if I hadn't been able to divorce a man I married when I was too young, or if my husband hadn't gotten divorced—for his sake and ultimately for mine. I'm just arguing against self-delusion. Just because a person wants to get divorced doesn't mean the children will be better off for it. They may be. They may not be. Divorce can leave young children with any number of deep emotional scars—a feeling that life is not safe, a distrust of love, a deep feeling of loss, fear of abandonment. Look at Alex's reaction to my impending departure.

I walked into the room where he was watching television. "I'm going to New York," I said.

"To live?" said Alex, eyes glued to the screen.

"Of course not. For a few days."

"Oh." Still no emotion.

It is Alex's style to be cool. "To live?" He asked the scary question not blinking an eye. It is Lisa's style to emote and throw herself in my arms. But both are expressing the same anxiety—fear of abandonment. Even though they have had consistent and devoted parenting since the separation (which was five years before this event), and even though Larry and I have been constantly and calmly together during that time (and their mother has had a stable life as well), they still feel vulnerable. Any departure might be an exit. They may resent my presence (Lisa more than Alex), but they certainly don't want me to leave. What a dilemma—to resent someone's presence but not be able to wish them good riddance for fear they might go. Not only would they miss me, but it would be further confirmation of their world's instability. They're confused emotionally because they don't trust permanence. That I'm the stepmother is not the poin. They would be ambivalent about a milkman if he were the next person after the divorce to walk into their lives and say, "Trust me."

Of course, my feelings about them are mixed up too. In fact, I'm beginning to feel that there is not a point of view we don't—or at least, that Lisa and I don't—share. I feel victimized; so does she. I feel left out; so does she. She feels ambivalent; well, me too. It's as though I'm looking in a mirror and seeing her reflection.

One night I took Alex to his Cub Scout meeting. I was feeling motherly. The scouts, their parents, and the scout leaders all sang a song about the Webelos, which means, "We will be loyal scouts."

"The Webelos are here,
The Webelos are here,
Stand up and take a bow,
The Webelos are here."

The leader then asked every scout to write down what he was thankful for, and I found myself thinking, Alex is going to put "my stepmother." What did he write? "My parents." I then spent some time wondering if that included me. I thought about how crazy I am about him; how I taught him to ride a bicycle; how I always carry his airplanes in my purse and once even carried around a ball of pizza dough, a souvenir of an Italian restaurant. I even sang the Webelo Song without flinching. But then I thought about how Alex always gets mixed up and calls his dad "Mom," on the day he switches from living at her house to living at ours. He never calls me Mom by mistake, or Dad either. The only person he mixes me up with is his teacher, whose name this year is Loretta. No, I concluded, in Alex's vocabulary, "parents" doesn't include me.

Then the scout leader passed around a sheet of paper for parents to sign up for volunteer committees—telephone, cleanup, etc. I thought, I don't have to do this. Let his parents do it. I even considered signing up Larry or his ex for the committee of my choice. What I'm saying is that, in regard to my stepchildren, I'm volatile. One minute I'm singing with all my heart; the next, my heart isn't in it. Usually, when I pull back, it's for protection. Then I'm less vulnerable to feeling neglected. I don't care as much that I have so little power, or that there are such constraints on my parenting or mothering. Of course, with all this ambivalence flying around, we—Lisa, Alex, and I—end up perpetually out of sync. Take my trip to New York. Just as I resigned myself to being thought of merely as useful, Lisa threw herself into my arms. I went in to see Alex, expecting love, and he acted self-protective.

There is a song that reminds me of my relationship with Lisa and Alex. It's by Stephen Sondheim, about lovers who can't connect. "Isn't it rich? Are we a pair? Me here at last on the ground, you in mid-air. . . . Send in the clowns."

Yes, this relationship needs some comic relief.

The comic relief a stepmother is most likely to summon is a child of her own. A new baby. This may not be too amusing to her stepchildren, but at least it cuts the tension of her relations with them. It takes her focus off it and solves a few problems—like her frustrated mothering—while it creates a few. My husband and I did not go that route for several reasons, including medical ones, age, and an attachment to a life which gave us family half the week and the life of a couple the other half. As complicated as joint custody is, it allows the delicious contradiction of having children and maintaining the intimacy of life before kids. So I have never "solved" my frustrations with stepmothering. I have just learned to live with them. Ironically, my life with Lisa and Alex has turned out to be about limits—not my setting them, but accepting them.

One day, about six years into stepmothering, Larry affectionately called me Dilky. Alex overheard, and I was never Delia again to him. Lisa hates Alex to have anything she doesn't have. "What did you call her?" she demanded. Then she was in on it too. So I became Dilky. They shout it down supermarket aisles, on street corners. Dilky, Dilky, Dilky. People turn around expecting to see a very large German hausfrau or a dachshund and there I am. I shouldn't complain. I have been adopted.

I have read articles in which six years is mentioned as a "magic number" when stepmother and stepchild finally settle in. Maybe it wouldn't take this long if the relationship started differently. The beginning, as far as I'm concerned, is the crux of the problem.

In the beginning there was the fountain, and the fountain had no water in it, and I told Lisa and Alex to get out. How absurd. Not that the fountain was empty, but that my first word as their future stepmother was "no." This little detail sums up the dumbness of stepmotherhood, or at least my approach to it. A mother begins with "yes." The baby is hungry. The mother feeds it. The baby cries. The mommy picks it up. The baby needs changing. Yes, yes, yes. The mommy builds the love and trust. Then one day the baby picks up an ashtray and starts to bean itself. "No," says the mother, and takes the ashtray away. But I started by seizing the ashtray. Under these circumstances, it's a miracle that the love came at all.

I have a favorite movie about stepmothering. It's a tearjerker called *Stella Dallas,* and I'm probably the only person who thinks stepmothering is what it's about. Made in the 1930s, it stars Barbara Stanwyck as Stella, a lower-class woman who marries up; Mr. Dallas is a refined, kind man whose quality she is too vulgar to recognize. After having a daughter, she ends up separated—a single mother before single mother was a group term.

In spite of her vulgarity, Stella has a good heart. She's just ignorant. She never learned social rules like "A woman should leave a party with the man she came with, especially if he's her husband." Stella dearly loves her daughter, Lollie, and wants her to have all the advantages. When Lollie becomes a teenager, Stella realizes that having a crass mother can only be a disadvantage. She gives Lollie up forever to her ex-husband and his incredibly kind, also refined, wife-to-be. Stella makes the greatest sacrifice a mother can make (and possibly the stupidest, but, as you will see, reality is never a concern in this movie). In the last scene, Stella's daughter is getting married and Stella is standing outside in the rain trying to glimpse the ceremony through the window. This is where everyone watching the movie cries. Not me. Here is where I cry:

Lollie's father, Stella's ex, is taking Lollie to meet his friend, the lovely widow. Lollie is very excited. It seems that she would rather meet this lady than spend the time alone with her father, even though she rarely sees him. She and her father enter a grand house, and the friend sweeps down the staircase. The father introduces her, saying, "This is Mrs. Morrison." Mrs. Morrison says, "Hello, Laurel, I'm so glad to see you." She takes Lollie's hand and clasps it to her heart. Then Lollie says—this is the amazing part—"I'm so glad to see you, too." She means it. She does not glare and say under her breath to her father, "No one calls me Laurel." She does not even pull her hand away. Then Mrs. Morrison says, "Michael, this is Laurel, whom we've been waiting and waiting to meet." And Michael, Mrs. Morrison's Great Dane (Lollie's future stepdog), jumps up on Lollie excitedly and begins licking her face.

Whenever I watch this scene, as I wipe my eyes, I think that if only Larry had introduced me to Lisa and Alex as Miss Ephron, everything would have gone smoothly.

Then Mrs. Morrison shows Lollie to her room. After a viewing of the canopy bed, Mrs. Morrison opens the closet. There, in the empty closet, hangs a neat row of satin-covered hangers with bows. Something about those hangers does me in. They symbolize the distance between that world and mine. A wood hanger is the fanciest hanger I have ever owned; mostly my hangers are wire. As I recall, the first time Lisa and Alex slept over at my place, they brought sleeping bags, and the need for hangers, wire or otherwise, never arose. Anyway, after I cry about that, I watch Lollie meet the boys, Mrs. Morrison's three sons, and I cry through several scenes in which they are all playing together and laughing. My favorite of these shows a game of Ping-Pong. Two boys are on one side of the table; Lollie and her father are on the other. The third boy is the ball boy and he's not complaining. He's not saying, "It's not fair. Before Lollie came, I got to play too!" No, he loves being the ball boy. It seems as if it's more of a treat for him than playing ever was.

The next thing you know, the boys are fighting for the privilege of carrying Lollie's luggage to the car, and as Lollie and her father drive away, her father asks her how she liked Mrs. Morrison. Lollie gushes. "I think she's the loveliest lady I ever knew." Then, flustered, realizing what she has said, she adds, "I mean, of course, I mean, except my mother."

Then there is this moment. Lollie's father and Mrs. Morrison are about to get married and Lollie has not locked herself in her bedroom with her hangers. She is sitting cozily on the couch and announces in a very pleased tone, "I never saw Father so happy before." Mrs. Morrison says, "And you, dear, are you happy?" Lollie gushes again, "So very, for you both." Imagine a child unqualifiedly happy for her father at his remarriage. And happy for his "friend." The idea is overwhelming. I have expected many things from my stepchildren, but not that they would delight in their father's and my happiness. As a child, I remember asking my parents over and over, "How did you meet?" I adored hearing the story of their romance. Lisa and Alex have never asked Larry or me that question, but if they did, I imagine their using a third-degree tone—like two detectives tracing a felony, our marriage, back to the moment the perpetrators met. So Lollie's enthusiasm at her father's happiness makes me weep for what can never be. But that is not the capper. The capper is this.

Stella knows Lollie is too devoted a child to leave her, so she tricks Lollie into believing that she wants to be rid of her. Lollie returns to her father, crying hysterically, and throws herself into his arms. At this point, Mrs. Morrison, now Lollie's stepmom, puts her arm around Lollie, too, and says, "Come upstairs with me, dear." And Lollie goes. She does not say, "No! I want to be with Daddy. I'm not your *dear!*" And I am weeping buckets, for in this scene the stepmother actually gets to mother.

Unfortunately, at that moment Lollie's boyfriend shows up and things get sidetracked. I would have liked a scene where the stepmother cheers Lollie up by making all her favorite foods and Lollie actually eats them. But Mrs. Morrison may not know how to cook since she has a cook.

I love this movie. It has absolutely nothing to do with my life. It imagines a second marriage with no baggage from the first. Mr. Dallas, Lollie, Mrs. Morrison, and her three boys are more harmonious than *Leave It to Beaver.* There is no possessiveness, jealousy, or anger. After Stella sends Lollie to live with her father permanently, she does not even telephone. Lollie suffers no adverse effects, and no one else in the family has to hear how Stella's car broke down or her hot water heater burst. What a romantic film—in the most contemporary way. My only complaint is, it shouldn't be called *Stella Dallas.* It should be called *Mrs. Morrison.*

The last time I saw this movie on television, I had my Kleenex out as Mrs. Morrison was saying to Lollie, "You're going to live with us." Lollie and Mrs. Morrison were sitting on the couch. It was just after Lollie's stepbrother had entrusted his prized goldfish to her care. At that moment my stepdaughter walked into the room and watched, puzzled, as Lollie said, "Live here?"

"The townhouse, wherever we are," said Mrs. Morrison.

"I don't get it. Who's that?" said Lisa.

"It's her stepmother," I said, through my tears.

"Do they like each other?" said Lisa.

"They love each other," I said, crying even harder.

Tales of
the Freeway

"My dad always drives in D-Three," said Lisa, and she reached over as I was driving 55 miles an hour on the San Bernadino Freeway and shifted the gear on the car.

At the time this happened, Larry, Lisa, Alex, and I were coming home from a weekend in the mountains. Lisa had just been given permission to sit in the front seat because she had a stomachache. (While the cause of the stomachache was certainly not the back seat, the cure might possibly be the front—such is the logic of parents.) It was about five minutes after being granted this treat that the outrage occurred.

Naturally I responded the way any sensible parent would: I started screaming. I was so angry that I have no memory of what I said. I assume that it was something along the lines of "Who do you think you are?" and "If you ever do that again . . ." In short, I threatened hysterically.

Lisa was stunned into silence, as was everyone else in the car. Dead silence for twenty minutes.

During this time I was completely wrecked. Almost paralyzed with anger, I stared fiercely at the road ahead. I was also beset with guilt. If Lisa did something this outrageous, I must somehow be responsible. I helped raise this child. Instantly I invoked my favorite defense, the stepmother's all-purpose out—"If she were my daughter, she wouldn't do this." For a change I might even be right, since this gear-shifting trick might be something Lisa would only try on her stepmother, might even be intended as a competitive gesture. On the other hand, knowing Lisa, she might do it to her mother too. I certainly would never have done anything like this to my mother. I have noticed that it is possible to have had the craziest relationship with your mother, and when your own child misbehaves, to become nostalgic for it. It's a sudden attack of jealousy for your mother's lot in life: She got to raise adorable me, and look what I get to raise—a wild child who shifts the gear of a moving car.

But what was bothering me most was the dread certainty: I-did-not-handle-this-correctly. When Lisa shifted the gear, I should have pulled over on the shoulder of the road and said calmly, in measured, firm tones, "Get into the back seat." Then I could have, once again calmly, scolded her, elucidating the terrifying possible consequences of her act. And then . . . I could have taken away her television for a week (or invoked some equally irrelevant punishment). What I should not have done was lose my temper. To lose your temper with a child is to feel the child has gotten the better of you. In this case, quite simply, my anger cured Lisa's stomachache and gave me one. Help!

Alex asked his dad if he would tell a story.

"Okay," said Larry. "I'm going to tell a story about a girl who couldn't control her impulses."

"Great," said Lisa.

"Once upon a time, there was a girl who couldn't control her impulses."

"What are impulses?" said Lisa.

"Whatever she wanted to do, she did. If she wanted to cry, she cried. If she wanted to laugh, she laughed. If she wanted to hit someone, she hit someone. If she wanted to shift the gear of the car, she shifted the gear of the car."

"Is this about me?" said Lisa.

"If the shoe fits, wear it."

"What does that mean?"

Larry explained. Lisa was silent.

"So go on, Dad," said Alex.

"The two parents consulted a doctor. 'Our daughter can't control her impulses,' they said. 'Can you help us?' The doctor said, 'For this problem, you need a specialist.' So they went to a specialist. 'Our daughter can't control her impulses.' 'I can't help you,' said the specialist. 'Go to a psychiatrist.' To expert after expert they went. They had just about given up when they finally came to a very old lady. 'Ha, ha, ha,' said the old lady. 'I know what to do.' And she gave the parents a roll of tape. 'What is this for?' said the parents. 'You figure it out,' said the old lady. And on the way home, it occurred to the parents what the tape was for. They taped the girl's mouth shut and her arms down, and after a week she was cured."

I loved that story. I loved Larry for making it up. How considerate of him to help me express my hostility. And it worked. I felt great. One teeny thing bothered me, though. Suppose Lisa thought that story meant it's okay to tape children up? Hmmm.

"I want to tell a story," said Lisa.

"Okay," said Larry.

"Once upon a time there was a boy who wanted to eat only junk food."

And she went on. It was a terrific story. It included everything he ate, mostly sugar, and his parents' frustration. The boy bore a strong resemblance to Alex, and, in the end, he blew up like a balloon from eating so much junk and floated away. He was never heard from again.

I was amazed by her story. Delighted. It is a great moment when your child chooses to learn the right thing in spite of your best efforts to confuse her. In this case, the range of conclusions Lisa could have drawn from Larry's story was considerable. On the one hand, we have

Tales of the Freeway

the possibility: Child abuse is okay, even effective. And on the other, we have the notion that an appropriate way to discharge anger is through fantasy. Content versus function. How sophisticated of Lisa to distinguish. How unexpected. What a relief. It's too bad she decided to show off her understanding by telling a story in which she disposed of her little brother. But still . . .

I pulled off the freeway feeling good, and, as I turned left, Alex spilled his grape juice all over the back seat of my new car.

"Alex, how could you?"

Larry interrupted. "Once upon a time there was a boy who spilled everything. His parents didn't know what to do. Finally God spoke to them and the house shook. God said, 'Get him a bottle.' "